MASTERING

ENGLISH GRAMMAR

£2

¹/04

D1634536

MACMILLAN MASTER SERIES

Astronomy
Australian History
Background to Business
Banking
Basic English Law
Basic Management
Biology
British Politics
Business Communication
Business Law
Business Microcomputing
Catering Science
Catering Theory
Chemistry
COBOL Programming
Commerce
Computer Programming
Computers
Data Processing
Economic and Social History
Economics
Electrical Engineering
Electronics
English Grammar
English Language
English Literature
Financial Accounting
French
French 2

German
Hairdressing
Italian
Italian 2
Japanese
Keyboarding
Marketing
Mathematics
Modern British History
Modern European History
Modern World History
Nutrition
Office Practice
Pascal Programming
Physics
Practical Writing
Principles of Accounts
Restaurant Service
Social Welfare
Sociology
Spanish
Spanish 2
Spreadsheets
Statistics
Statistics with your Microcomputer
Study Skills
Typewriting Skills
Word Processing

OTHER BOOKS BY S. H. BURTON INCLUDE

Comprehension Practice
English Study and Composition
Modern Précis Practice
A Comprehensive English Course
People and Communication
Mastering English Language
The Criticism of Poetry
The Criticism of Prose

MASTERING
ENGLISH GRAMMAR

S. H. BURTON

MACMILLAN

© S. H. Burton 1984

All rights reserved. No reproduction, copy or transmission
of this publication may be made without written permission.

No paragraph of this publication may be reproduced, copied
or transmitted save with written permission or in accordance
with the provisions of the Copyright Act 1956 (as amended),
or under the terms of any licence permitting limited copying
issued by the Copyright Licensing Agency, 33—4 Alfred Place,
London WC1E 7DP.

Any person who does any unauthorised act in relation to
this publication may be liable to criminal prosecution and
civil claims for damages.

First published 1984
Reprinted 1985, 1986, 1987, 1989

Published by
MACMILLAN EDUCATION LTD
Houndmills, Basingstoke, Hampshire RG21 2XS
and London
Companies and representatives
throughout the world

Printed in Hong Kong

British Library Cataloguing in Publication Data
Burton, S. H.
Mastering English grammar.
1. English language — Grammar — 1950—
I. Title
428.2   PE1112
ISBN 0—333—36367—1
ISBN 0—333—36368—X Pbk
ISBN 0—333—36369—8 Pbk export

CONTENTS

Preface			ix
Acknowledgement			x
1 What is grammar?	1.1	Language and communication	1
	1.2	Making sense	1
	1.3	Grammar and sense	2
2 Phrases and sentences	2.1	Word groups	4
	2.2	Phrases	4
	2.3	Sentences	5
	2.4	Four kinds of sentences	7
	2.5	The punctuation of written sentences	8
3 Subject and predicate	3.1	The two parts of the sentence	10
	3.2	The functions of the two parts	11
	3.3	Subject and predicate (1)	12
	3.4	Subject and predicate (2)	13
4 Words in sentences	4.1	Words at work	19
	4.2	Different work for the same word	20
5 An introduction to the parts of speech	5.1	The eight parts of speech	22
	5.2	Nouns	23
	5.3	Verbs	25
	5.4	Pronouns	29
	5.5	Adjectives	30
	5.6	Adverbs	33
	5.7	Prepositions	38
	5.8	Conjunctions	41
	5.9	Interjections	42
	5.10	Family groups and word behaviour	43
6 The parts of the simple sentence	6.1	Definition of the simple sentence	44
	6.2	Subject and predicate	45
	6.3	The subject and the subject-word	45

CONTENTS

	6.4	Subject-word and words qualifying subject-word	46
	6.5	Predicate: the verb and words modifying the verb	47
	6.6	Predicate: the direct object	48
	6.7	Predicate: the indirect object	50
	6.8	Predicate: predicative words (or complement)	52
	6.9	A tabular list of all the parts of the simple sentence	54
7 Finite verbs and non-finite verbs	7.1	Finite verbs	56
	7.2	Non-finite verbs	58
	7.3	Participial phrases	63
	7.4	Gerundive phrases	65
	7.5	Infinitive phrases	66
8 Simple sentence analysis	8.1	Tabular analysis	68
	8.2	Descriptive analysis	69
	8.3	Graphic analysis	72
	8.4	Analysing phrases	76
9 Clauses and sentences	9.1	What is a clause?	82
	9.2	Main clauses	83
	9.3	Co-ordinating conjunctions	83
	9.4	Double sentences	83
	9.5	Multiple sentences	85
	9.6	Complex sentences	86
	9.7	Kinds of sentences: a check-list	87
	9.8	Summing up	88
10 Subordinate clauses and the work they do	10.1	Introduction	89
	10.2	Adjective-clauses	90
	10.3	Adverb-clauses	95
	10.4	Noun-clauses	101
11 The analysis of complex, double and multiple sentences	11.1	Method	105
	11.2	Procedure	106
	11.3	Notes on procedure	106
	11.4	Worked examples: complex sentences	107

		11.5	Double and multiple sentence analysis	110
		11.6	Tests in analysis	113
12	The parts of speech: a chapter for reference	12.1	Introduction	115
		12.2	Nouns	116
		12.3	Pronouns	119
		12.4	Adjectives	121
		12.5	Verbs	124
		12.6	Adverbs	137
		12.7	Prepositions	139
		12.8	Conjunctions	140
		12.9	Interjections	140
		12.10	'It' as a provisional subject	140
		12.11	'There' as an introductory adverb	141
13	Common errors and debatable points	13.1	Introduction	142
		13.2	Agreement	142
		13.3	Case	149
		13.4	Verb-forms	152
		13.5	The rule of proximity	153
		13.6	Woolly use of pronouns	155
		13.7	Defining and non-defining phrases and clauses	156
		13.8	Chopping and changing	157
		13.9	Tests	158

Answers to tests — 160

Index — 175

PREFACE

This book is an exploration of the behaviour of English words in English sentences. All the grammatical terms and concepts necessary to a thorough understanding of the simple sentence are first explained and illustrated, for the simple sentence is the bedrock on which fluent, accurate and elegant English expression is based.

Later, the more intricate structures of double, multiple, and complex sentences are examined. Those sentences are enlargements of the simple sentence and they are well made when they conform to its basic patterns.

I must emphasise that Chapter 12 *is* what it is called: a chapter for reference. It supplies information about grammatical terms that you may need to look up; and it gathers together the facts that are treated at length and in the course of discussion throughout the rest of the book. A source of quick reference is useful, but it is a back-up to, not a substitute for, the expositions given elsewhere.

Grammar cannot explain everything. The English language is living, changing, flexible. Some of its nimble improvisations defy precise explanations. Yet that seems no sound argument for rejecting the very considerable help that grammar can give. I believe that this grammar book will help you as you use the language.

S. H. BURTON

ACKNOWLEDGEMENT

The author and publishers are grateful for permission to reproduce cartoons from *The Complete Molesworth*, copyright © 1958 by Ronald Searle.

WHAT IS GRAMMAR?

1.1 LANGUAGE AND COMMUNICATION

Every day of our lives we send spoken or written messages to other people, and every day we receive spoken or written messages from other people. These two activities occupy a lot of our time at home, in our social life outside the family, and at work.

Simply because we are human beings who live and work with other human beings, communication (message sending and receiving) plays an inescapable and all-important part in our lives.

It is possible to communicate without using words. We can shake our head instead of saying, 'No'. We can smile instead of saying, 'I am pleased'. We can frown instead of saying, 'I don't like that'. Yet, though we all make use of non-verbal signs, the fact remains that messages without words are strictly limited in their scope, totally inadequate to serve any but the simplest purposes. We could not get through a day's living with any satisfaction or success if we were able to communicate only by means of nods, smiles, frowns, gestures and grunts.

If we could not send and receive spoken and written messages we should be cut off from our fellow human beings. Communication above the most primitive level depends upon the use of language.

1.2 MAKING SENSE

In the course of a single day we need to exchange messages of many different kinds with many different people. To do that successfully, we have to know a lot of words and we have to be able to choose the right words to suit each separate message: efficient communication requires a large vocabulary.

However, using language is not just a matter of knowing words and knowing which words to use. Our ability to make ourselves understood in any language, whether it is our native language or a foreign language, depends on two things:

- First, we have to know the words that will express whatever it is we are trying to express.
- Second, we have to know how words behave in the particular language we are trying to use.

Knowing the words is vital, of course; but knowing the words is not much use *on its own*. For example, we may know the French words for a message that we are trying to send in French, but no French person will be able to understand us if the words of our message do not behave in the ways that the French language requires.

That is true of every language. If we are speaking or writing German, we must make our words behave in the ways of the German language. Russian words must behave in Russian ways, English words in English ways, and so on.

Every language has its own special ways of making words behave. If the words of any message, spoken or written, do not behave in the ways required by that language, the message cannot make sense.

1.3 GRAMMAR AND SENSE

As we have just seen, every language has its own particular ways of making words behave.

- The particular kinds of word behaviour that a particular language demands are what we call the *grammar* of that language.

So, when we say that English grammar is different from French grammar, that is simply another way of saying that the behaviour of words in the English language is different from the behaviour of words in the French language.

English speakers learning French must learn to recognise and copy the word behaviour of the French language. That is to say, they must learn, and learn how to use, French grammar. French speakers learning English must learn to recognise and copy the word behaviour of the English language. That is to say, they must learn, and learn how to use, English grammar.

Because the grammars of the two languages are different, it is no use trying to make English behave like French, or French behave like English. Neither language can work with any grammar but its own; and we cannot make ourselves understood in either language if we use the wrong grammar.

Whether we are speaking or writing in a foreign language *or in our own language*, our use of words must obey the grammatical rules of that

CHAPTER 2

PHRASES AND SENTENCES

2.1 WORD GROUPS

Very young children use single words when they speak, but they soon out-grow that inefficient way of communicating. They learn how to make themselves understood by using words in groups. The response that they get from other people teaches them which of the word groups they are using make sense and which do not. In this way they progress, learning language skills by trial and error until they can frame word groups that make complete sense.

- Words are the building blocks of language. Until we can build words up into meaningful groups and make meaningful connections between one group of words and another, we cannot use language efficiently.
- The study of grammar is essentially the study of how words behave in groups. Grammar explains the relationships between one word and another and the relationships between one group of words and another.

2.2 PHRASES

Not all word groups make *complete* sense. Here are some examples of word groups that do not:

during her holiday
after my twenty-first birthday
considering his injury
in that street
beneath the foundations

Each of those word groups makes *some* sense. No English-speaking person would dismiss any of them as nonsense, but in every case the meaning is incomplete. None of them can stand alone.

- Word groups such as those are *phrases*.

Although a phrase cannot make complete sense on its own, it can be used as part of a word group that does make complete sense. Like this:

1 Our neighbour wrote several postcards *during her holiday.*
2 I was given a pay rise *after my twenty-first birthday.*
3 *Considering his injury*, he played a remarkable game.
4 We saw two empty houses *in that street.*
5 The ground shifted *beneath the foundations.*

Phrases play a very important part in our use of language, and we shall study their grammatical function in detail later. For the moment, it is sufficient to be able to recognise a phrase and to understand how it differs from a sentence.

2.3 SENTENCES

In Section 2.2 we saw that a phrase can be added to another word group with the result that the *incomplete* sense of the phrase becomes part of the *complete* sense of the larger word group. Like this:

1 OUR NEIGHBOUR WROTE SEVERAL POSTCARDS *during her holiday.*
2 I WAS GIVEN A PAY RISE *after my twenty-first birthday.*
3 *Considering his injury*, HE PLAYED A REMARKABLE GAME.
4 WE SAW TWO EMPTY HOUSES *in that street.*
5 THE GROUND SHIFTED *beneath the foundations.*

Notice this very important fact. The word groups (in capitals) to which the phrases (in italics) have been added do not need the phrases in the way that the phrases need them, The phrases *add* something to the meaning of the word groups to which they are joined, but they do not *complete* their meaning.

The word groups in capitals can stand alone. They make complete sense without the help of the phrases:

OUR NEIGHBOUR WROTE SEVERAL POSTCARDS.
I WAS GIVEN A PAY RISE.
HE PLAYED A REMARKABLE GAME.
WE SAW TWO EMPTY HOUSES.
THE GROUND SHIFTED.

Word groups such as these are *sentences*.

REMEMBER

- A sentence is a group of words that makes complete sense.
- It can stand on its own without needing any additional words to complete its meaning.

6

- It is an independent, self-contained, completely understandable utterance.

Test 1

Answers on page 160.

Which of the following word groups are sentences and which are phrases?

1 The old man sat down.
2 In his comfortable armchair.
3 He was tired.
4 After his walk.
5 He switched on his radio.
6 Then he lit his pipe.
7 With a match.
8 The music on the radio soothed him.
9 He forgot his pipe.
10 It went out.
11 He slept.
12 For nearly an hour.
13 At last.
14 The telephone woke him.

Test 2

Suggested answers on page 160. When you have written your answers compare them with my suggestions, just to make sure that you are on the right lines.

Use each of these phrases as part of a sentence.

Example

Phrase   by early morning
Sentence By early morning the fog had cleared.

1 at the end of the street
2 after dark
3 in turns
4 through a silly mistake
5 by violent means
6 judging by the results
7 without permission
8 for the present

2.4 FOUR KINDS OF SENTENCES

All sentences make complete sense on their own, but not all sentences do the same kind of work.

Consider these four sentences:

1 We have enough coal for this winter.
2 Are you sure?
3 Look in the cellar.
4 What a lot you have bought!

Sentence 1 makes a *statement*.
Sentence 2 asks a *question*.
Sentence 3 gives a *command*.
Sentence 4 utters an *exclamation*.

Sentences can perform four different functions: make statements, ask questions; give commands; utter exclamations.

Test 3
Answers on page 160.
Classify each of the following sentences according to the work that it does (statement; question; command; exclamation).

1 Tests are a good way of revising.
2 We have to answer the questions.
3 Did you pass the examination?
4 Rule a line under that heading.
5 The paper was difficult.
6 It was a brute!
7 That book helped me a lot.
8 Who recommended it?
9 I read about it in the paper.
10 The local bookshop ordered it for me.

Test 4
Suggested answers (for comparison with yours) on page 160.
Write four sentences on each of the following topics: sewing; cooking; reading. Your sentences must be in this order: (i) a statement; (ii) a question; (iii) a command; (iv) an exclamation.

Example

Topic bicycles

Sentence (i)   That model has ten gears.   (*statement*)

Sentence (ii)	Are ten gears a help?	*(question)*
Sentence (iii)	Ride the bike for a few miles.	*(command)*
Sentence (iv)	What a difference the gears make!	*(exclamation)*

2.5 THE PUNCTUATION OF WRITTEN SENTENCES

Because a sentence is a group of words that makes complete sense *on its own*, it is necessary to mark off each sentence from the others when we are writing. If the beginning and the end of each separate and complete thought were not clearly indicated, the reader would be confused.

REMEMBER

- A *statement* sentence must begin with a capital letter and end with a full stop.
- A *question* sentence must begin with a capital letter and end with a question mark.
- A *command* sentence must begin with a capital letter and it usually ends with a full stop. If the command is short and sharp, however, it usually ends with an exclamation mark. (*Shut up! Come quickly!*)
- An *exclamation* sentence must begin with a capital letter and end with and exclamation mark.

Test 5
Answers on page 160.
Rewrite the following jumbled sentences. Insert the necessary capital letters and full stops so that each separate and complete thought is marked off from the others.

1 the film was a good one it kept closely to the facts of the historical events on which it was based
2 by half-time it was clear that we were going to win our forwards were stronger and faster than theirs
3 on a very cold morning frost crystals appear on the windows their beauty is some compensation for our discomfort
4 the bus was late in starting we missed morning assembly that day
5 the beech keeps its leaves longer than most other trees its autumn colours last well into winter often they are still there in early spring

Test 6
Answer on page 161.
Punctuate this passage correctly. You will need to supply capital letters, full stops, question marks and one exclamation mark.

do you understand the difference between sentences and phrases it is important to be clear about it making complete sense depends on being able to frame sentences think hard about punctuation, too this passage is not easy to understand why isn't it it's a jumble the writer has forgotten to punctuate

SUBJECT AND PREDICATE

REMEMBER

- A sentence is a group of words that expresses a complete thought. Unlike a phrase, it can stand alone and make full sense without the help of any additional words.

3.1 THE TWO PARTS OF THE SENTENCE

Every sentence consists of two parts. Here are ten examples in which the two parts of each sentence are printed in such a way as to mark each part off from the other.

1 OUR NEIGHBOUR *wrote several postcards.*
2 I *was given a pay rise after my twenty-first birthday.*
3 HE *played a remarkable game.*
4 WE *saw two empty houses.*
5 THE GROUND *shifted.*
6 JOHN *ran across the street.*
7 THE LITTLE BOY *ate a sweet.*
8 THE AEROPLANE *dived steeply.*
9 HENS *lay eggs.*
10 THE USE OF LANGUAGE *distinguishes human beings from the other animals.*

As you can see, *both* parts are necessary. Take away either and the part that is left does not express a complete thought. In other words, if either part is missing, the part that is left is *not* a sentence.

Examples

1 OUR NEIGHBOUR . . . does not express a complete thought. Therefore, it is not a sentence.

2 . . .*wrote several postcards* does not express a complete thought. There-fore, it is not a sentence.

3 HE. . . does not express a complete thought. Therefore, it is not a sentence.

4 . . .*played a remarkable game* does not express a complete thought. Therefore, it is not a sentence.

3.2 THE FUNCTIONS OF THE TWO PARTS

Consider this sentence:

1	2
Our neighbour	wrote several postcards.

Part 1 (Our neighbour) names the person about whom something is being said.

Part 2 (wrote several postcards) says something about the person named in Part 1.

Similarly:

1	2
He	played a remarkable game.

Part 1 (He) names the person about whom something is being said.

Part 2 (played a remarkable game) says something about the person named in Part 1.

Another example:

1	2
The use of language	distinguishes human beings from the other animals.

Part 1 (The use of language) names the idea about which something is being said.

Part 2 (distinguishes human beings from the other animals) says something about the idea named in Part 1.

- Every sentence consists of two parts.
- One part names the person, thing or idea about which something is being said.
- One part says something about the person, thing or idea named by the other part.

3.3 SUBJECT AND PREDICATE (1)

That part of a sentence which *names* the person, idea or thing about which something is being said is called the *subject* of the sentence.

That part of a sentence which says something about the person, idea or thing named by the subject is called the *predicate* of the sentence.

- Every sentence contains both a subject and a predicate.

Examples

	Subject	Predicate
1	Our neighbour	wrote several postcards.
2	He	played a remarkable game.
3	The use of language	distinguishes human beings from the other animals.
4	Every sentence	contains both a subject and a predicate.

You will find it easy to remember the functions of the subject and the predicate if you think about the meanings of the two terms.

The *subject* names the person, thing or idea about which something is being said. A sensible term, for the *subject* announces the subject of the sentence: who or what it is about.

The *predicate* says something about the person, thing or idea named by the subject. Another sensible term, if you remember that it comes from a Latin word meaning *to declare*. So the *predicate* declares/states something about the subject named by the *subject*.

REMEMBER

To frame a sentence, you must
- name your subject (provide a *subject* for your sentence)
- say something about your subject (provide a *predicate* for your sentence)

Unless you do both, the group of words you have framed is *not* a sentence, for it does not express a complete thought.

Test 7

Answers on page 161.

Identify the subject and predicate in each of these sentences.

1 This test is the seventh in this book.
2 Most readers will have no trouble in answering.
3 Studying sentences is the main activity of grammar.
4 Subject and predicate must be identified.
5 The term 'predicate' comes from a Latin word meaning 'to declare'.

Test 8

Suggested answers on page 161.

Use each of the following as the predicate of a sentence. Try to supply an interesting subject for each, avoiding dull and obvious answers. For example, it would not be very enterprising to supply 'he' or 'we' or 'they' as a subject for 1.

1 . . .reached a record-breaking speed.
2 . . .examined my swollen hand.
3 . . .were exhausted after their polar journey.
4 . . .identified the comet.
5 . . .tried to arrange a cease-fire.

Test 9

Suggested answers on page 161.

Use each of the following as the subject of a sentence, supplying an interesting and appropriate predicate.

1 The first day of the new term. . .
2 The Suez Canal. . .
3 Grammatical errors. . .
4 Malaria. . .
5 Air travel. . .

3.4 SUBJECT AND PREDICATE (2)

(a) Subject/predicate order

In English, the subject of the sentence usually precedes the predicate, like this:

Subject	Predicate
The subject	usually precedes the predicate.

The normal subject/predicate order can be *inverted*, with the result that the predicate precedes the subject, like this:

Predicate	Subject
1 With a few strokes was felled	that ancient tree.
2 Never to her childhood home returned	the sad exile.
3 Far from the shore could be glimpsed	the stricken vessel.

In sentences of that pattern, the normal sentence order is reversed, with the intention of emphasising the words in the predicate. They attract attention to themselves because they appear in an unexpected place in the sentence. The subject and the predicate are wrenched around to surprise the reader.

Inversion (predicate preceding subject) is employed *only* for special effects in dramatic and narrative prose and in verse, and very sparingly at that. It is an abnormal and artificial device, out of place in good, clear English prose.

A *modified* form of inversion, however, is common. In many well-made English sentences, *part* of the predicate precedes the subject. Such frequently-used sentences have this construction:

part of predicate	subject	rest of predicate

Examples

1 In her retirement, the ex-prime minister wrote her autobiography.
Subject   the ex-prime minister
Predicate   wrote her autobiography in her retirement
2 By that time, the explorers were reduced to their last rations.
Subject   the explorers
Predicate   were reduced to their last rations by that time
3 In English, the subject of the sentence normally precedes the predicate.
Subject   the subject of the sentence
Predicate   normally precedes the predicate in English

This modified form of inversion is a frequent pattern in *exclamation* sentences.

Examples

1 How dangerous that chimney looks!
Subject   that chimney
Predicate   looks how dangerous
2 What a time we had!
Subject   we
Predicate   had what a time

(b) Subject and predicate in question sentences

So far, we have concentrated on statement and exclamation sentences. When analysing question sentences, the method of finding the subject and predicate is first to convert the question sentence into a statement, like this:

1 Are you hungry? converts into *You are hungry.*
Subject   You
Predicate   are hungry
2 Have you brought sandwiches? converts into *You have brought sandwiches.*
Subject   You
Predicate   have brought sandwiches
3 Are they beef sandwiches? converts into *They are beef sandwiches.*
Subject   They
Predicate   are beef sandwiches
4 Do you like them? converts into *You do like them.*
Subject   You
Predicate   do like them
4 Are the sandwiches in the tin? converts into *The sandwiches are in the tin.*
Subject   The sandwiches
Predicate   are in the tin

(c) The 'understood' subject

Often, the subject of a command sentence is not expressed, though both the giver of the command and its receiver understand very well who the subject is.

Examples

1 Lend me your umbrella.
2 Bring the spanners.
3 Don't touch that switch.
4 Be careful!
5 Keep quiet!

A group of words constructed on that pattern makes complete sense because, though the subject is not explicitly named, the giver of the command and the receiver understand who the subject is.

When we analyse such sentences, we supply the missing subject. It is called the 'understood' subject:

1 Lend me your umbrella.
Subject   (You)

Predicate lend me your umbrella
2 Bring the spanners.
Subject (You)
Predicate bring the spanners

Test 10

Answers on page 161.
Analyse the rest of those above examples into subject and predicate, remembering to enclose the 'understood' subject in brackets.

(d) One-word sentences

Although most sentences consists of more than one word, it is perfectly possible to speak or write one-word sentences. Command sentences often consist of one word, like this:

1 Stop!
Subject (You)
Predicate stop
2 Sit!
Subject (You)
Predicate sit

One-word exclamation and question sentences have an 'understood' subject and part of the predicate is also 'understood'.

Examples

Exclamation sentences
1 Rubbish!
Subject (That)
Predicate (is) rubbish
2 Ass!
Subject (You)
Predicate (are) (an) ass

Question sentences
1 Ready?
Subject (You)
Predicate (are) ready
2 All right?
Subject (You)
Predicate (are) all right

Faced with the sentence 'All right?' on its own, we can, of course, assign alternative meanings to it. For example, it could mean, 'Am I doing this all right?' In that case, the analysis would be:

All right?
Subject   (I)
Predicate (am) (doing) (this) all right

A one-word sentence usually occurs in a context that establishes which meaning it carries. Out of context, we cannot be certain which of several possible meanings it has.

The *grammatical* point, however, is entirely clear: a one-word sentence has an 'understood' subject; and *part of* its predicate may also be 'understood'.

Test 11
Answers on page 162.
State which of the following are sentences. Identify each sentence as either a statement, a question, a command, or an exclamation.

1 Into the valley of death.
2 Into the valley of death rode the six hundred.
3 Write this down at once.
4 Can you see the summit?
5 For five hours or more.
6 They climbed steadily for five hours or more.
7 Switch on your oxygen set.
8 He switched it on immediately.
9 Is there enough oxygen?
10 How precious the supply was!

Test 12
Suggested answers on page 162.
Write out the question sentences to which the following would be sensible answers.

1 I should like a book.
2 Adventure stories are my favourites.
3 No, I'm not very fond of short stories.
4 At eleven o'clock, I think.
5 They missed their bus.

Test 13
Suggested answers on page 162.
Invent command sentences appropriate to these situations.

1 Your dog, whose paws are muddy, is jumping up to greet you.
2 Someone with whom you are arguing is getting angry.
3 Your brother/sister has borrowed your bicycle.

4 A ticket collector has entered a railway coach in which you are travelling.
5 You are sending a child on an errand.

Test 14
Answers on page 162.
Analyse (divide) the following sentences into subject and predicate.

1 Horace hit his hand with a hammer.
2 Tuesday night's programmes are better than Wednesday's.
3 With a courage born of desperation, he flung himself at his enemies.
4 Slowly and painfully, they worked out the answers.
5 Happy?
6 Put it down.
7 Idiot!
8 Have you cleaned your shoes?
9 Reading is one of my favourite pleasures.
10 Jean has used the last of the shampoo.

WORDS IN SENTENCES

4.1 WORDS AT WORK

Words do not work as single, self-contained units of meaning. They work in groups. The efficiency with which we can use language depends on our ability to arrange individual words in meaningful groups and to establish meaningful connections between the word groups that we have built up.

The most important unit of meaning is the sentence, for it is a group of words that expresses complete sense within its own boundaries. It is an independent utterance that does not require the addition of any other words to complete its meaning.

Each word in a sentence does its own particular job. It performs a particular function in the sentence in which it is used and, at the same time, it relates to other words in the same sentence.

To illustrate that point, here are examples of *some* of the jobs that words can do in sentences and *some* of the ways in which they can relate to each other.

Sentence 1

Hilda and her mother walked quickly.

Word	Function in sentence 1
Hilda mother	*name* persons
walked	tells us what the persons already named *did* – denotes an *action* – functions as an 'action word'
quickly	*describes* the *manner* in which the *action* was performed
her	*describes* the person named by the word 'mother – indicates *whose* mother is referred to
and	*connects* two words ('Hilda', 'mother')

Sentence 2

Wholemeal bread is healthy food.

Word	Function in sentence 2
bread ⎱ food ⎰	*name* things
is	denotes the *state of being* of one of the things already named ('bread') – functions as a 'being word'
wholemeal	*describes* the thing named by the word 'bread'
healthy	*describes* the thing named by the word 'food'

The functions of the words in those two sentences were described in every-day terms. Those terms were not always well suited to that task, but they had one advantage. Their use emphasised the everyday applications of the study of grammar. Grammar is not a remote, academic study. It is a practical subject, concerned with our daily use of language. It teaches us to look at words in sentences *analytically*, discovering what each word is doing and how sentences are built. By helping us to understand how sentences are made it helps us to use our language better.

A careful analytical examination of those two sentences enabled us to give an accurate – if rather unwieldy – account of the job done by each word and to indicate the relationships between words.

The accepted grammatical terms for word functions will be introduced in Chapter 5. They are clear, exact and economical; and they provide the vocabulary that we need to give a precise account of the ways in which words work in sentences.

4.2 DIFFERENT WORK FOR THE SAME WORD

Before we go on to study the meaning and use of those grammatical terms, however, we must be clear about a bedrock fact of grammar. It is this:

- The grammatical function of an isolated word cannot be determined. We do not know what work a word does until we examine the part that it plays in the sentence to which it belongs. A word may perform one function in one sentence and a different function in another.

Examples

1 Our sails were torn by the ferocious storms.
2 This yacht sails best in stiff breezes.
3 They say she storms at her husband in public.
4 If they husband their resources they should survive.

In those four sentences there are three examples of words that change their grammatical functions from one sentence to another:

In sentence 1 'sails' is a *naming word.*
In sentence 2 'sails' is an *action word.*
In sentence 1 'storms' is a *naming word.*
In sentence 3 'storms' is an *action word.*
In sentence 3 'husband' is a *naming word.*
In sentence 4 'husband' is an *action word.*

Test 15
Suggested answers on page 162.
Use each of these words in two sentences in such a way that it has a different grammatical function in each sentence. When you have written out your answers, compare them with mine to check that you are thinking along the right lines.

1   park   2   down   3   colour   4   knife   5   break

REMEMBER

• Grammatically speaking, a word *is* what it *does* in a sentence. So, for example, the same word can function as a *naming word* in one sentence and as an *action word* in another.

CHAPTER 5

AN INTRODUCTION TO THE PARTS OF SPEECH

5.1 THE EIGHT PARTS OF SPEECH

In Section 4.1 we studied two sentences and described each word in each sentence in terms of the work that it did in the sentence. We saw that 'Hilda', 'mother', 'bread' and 'food' were *naming words* in those sentences, 'walked' was an *action word*, 'healthy' was a *describing word* – describing the thing named by the word 'food' – and so on.

Those were accurate accounts of the various word functions, but they were clumsy. If that method of describing the work that words do were adopted for longer and more complicated sentences, the descriptions would become intolerably long-winded. That is why we need to know the accepted grammatical terms. Those terms are precise and immediately understood.

When we classify a word according to its function in a sentence we describe it as being a particular 'part of speech'.

REMEMBER

- The parts of speech are the classes into which words are placed *according to the work that they do in a sentence.*

There are *eight* parts of speech; their names are: *noun*; *verb*; *pronoun*; *adjective*; *adverb*; *preposition*; *conjunction*; *interjection*.

Each word in a sentence can be classified *by its function* as being one or the other of those eight parts of speech.

It is not necessary at this early stage of grammatical study to discuss the parts of speech in full detail. Further particulars of classification will be dealt with when we move on to the study of *complex sentences*. You will find all the necessary information in Chapters 9 to 12.

Our immediate concern is with the fundamental facts of grammar. The information given in this chapter is the essential minimum needed to study the grammar of the *simple sentence*.

5.2 NOUNS

The English word 'noun' comes from the Latin word *nomen*, meaning 'name'.

- The function of a noun is to *name* someone or something.

Examples

1 *Helen* wrote to *Jean*.
2 *Justice* need not exclude *mercy*.
3 A *crowd* gathered to watch the *fleet* sail.
4 His *father* bought him a *bicycle*.

There are two nouns in each of those sentences, and each pair is an example of a different kind of noun.

1	Helen	Jean:	*proper* nouns
2	justice	mercy:	*abstract* nouns
3	crowd	fleet:	*collective* nouns
4	father	bicycle:	*common* nouns

Proper nouns name a *particular* person, place or thing. For example: Helen, Jean, Europe, London, Christmas, Canada, British Broadcasting Corporation.

The word 'proper' comes from the Latin word *proprius*, meaning 'own'. So a *proper noun* denotes the 'own name' of a particular person, place or thing.

The name *girl* is the name that Helen shares with a whole class of human beings, but the name *Helen* belongs to her personally. The name *continent* is the name that Europe shares with other land masses, but the name *Europe* is its own name. The BBC shares the name *corporation* with thousands of other similar organisations, but its own particular name is *British Broadcasting Corporation*.

REMEMBER

- Proper nouns, when written, begin with a capital letter.

Abstract nouns name qualities or states of being that exist only in our minds. For example: cleverness, courage, happiness, humility, justice, loyalty, mercy, sorrow, wisdom.

All the other kinds of nouns name people, places or things that have a material existence. Abstract nouns name non-material things: intangible states of mind, qualities and feelings.

Collective nouns name groups of people or collections of things regarded as a whole. For example: crew, crowd, fleet, forest, library, team. Every collective noun names a group or collection of individual units. A crew is composed of sailors; a crowd is composed of people; a fleet is composed of ships; a forest is composed of trees, and so on.

Common nouns name members of or items in a whole class of people or things. For example: bicycle, brother, father, man, nest, party, pencil, riot, ship, sister, woman.

You may come across the term *concrete* or *material nouns*, referring to things like: cotton, nylon, rubber, silk, water. Such nouns behave like all other common nouns, so there seems little point in making them a special subdivision of common nouns.

REMEMBER

1 When a word functions as a 'naming word' it is a noun.
2 Since the subject of a sentence *names* the person, thing, or idea about which the sentence is saying something, it follows that there must always be a 'naming word' in the subject of a sentence. That 'naming word' is a noun or a pronoun – see Section 5.4.

Test 16
Answers on page 163.
There are fourteen nouns in the following sentences. Seven are proper nouns; the rest are common nouns. Pick out each noun and say what kind it is.

1 Henry scored plenty of runs that day.
2 They landed at Southampton in July and toured England by car.
3 My cat is called Hodge.
4 That novel was written by Dickens.
5 My birthday falls on a Tuesday this year.

Test 17
Answers on page 163.
With two exceptions the nouns in the following passage are all of one kind. Pick out each noun and say what kind it is.

His second son fell sick, and he removed him to one of the upper rooms, which he had set aside as a hospital, and attended upon him himself. In a few days, however, his fears were removed and he found, to his great satisfaction, that the youth had not been attacked by the plague, but was only suffering from a slight fever, which quickly yielded to the remedies applied.

Test 18

Answers on page 163.

List all the nouns in the following sentences and classify them as common or abstract.

1 The engine was brilliantly designed to achieve maximum quietness at high revolutions.
2 He had no friends or relations and lived in solitude.
3 As a player, his sportsmanship was outstanding.
4 We were rivals, but I felt no enmity for her.
5 Even when she was old, her beauty was remarkable.

Test 19

Answers on page 163.

List the collective nouns in the following sentences.

1 Their navy consists of over sixty ships.
2 We elected a new committee early in the year.
3 The shepherds drove their flocks from the hills.
4 There are nearly two hundred components in that kit.
5 The bad weather dispersed the shoals.

Test 20

Answers on page 163.

Nouns of every kind are used in this sentence. Identify each.

My friend Smith was a member of the team that played with such courage to win the cup.

5.3 VERBS

As we have seen in Sections 3.3 and 3.4, the predicate of a sentence says something about the subject of that sentence. There can be no sentence without a predicate, just as there can be no sentence without a subject. Each of the two parts of the sentence requires the other in order to express a complete thought.

(a) The essential word in the predicate

In the predicate of every sentence, one word (or group of words) plays the essential part in telling us something about the subject of the sentence.

Examples

Subject	Predicate
1 The detective	*found* three witnesses.
2 My sister	*emptied* the bag of sweets.
3 A rescue team	*reached* the stranded climbers.

If the italicised word is omitted from each of these sentences, the words that remain no longer form a sentence, for they do not express a complete thought:

1 The detective - three witnesses
2 My sister - the bag of sweets
3 A rescue team - the stranded climbers

REMEMBER

• The word (or group of words) that performs the essential 'telling' function in the predicate is called the *verb*.

The word 'verb' comes from the Latin word *verbum*, meaning 'the word'. That is a useful clue to the importance of the work that the verb does. The verb is '*the* word' in the predicate.

Such is the importance of the verb, that a predicate may consist solely of one word - a verb.

Examples

Subject	Predicate
1 Fish	swim.
2 Wet timbers	rot.
3 Over-stressed girders	collapse.

REMEMBER

• A predicate cannot function without a verb.

(b) 'Action words' and 'being words'
The verbs used in the examples in Section 5.3(a) all functioned as 'action words': found, emptied, reached, swim, rot, collapse. Though many verbs have that function, some do not.

Examples

1 Tom Bradley *is* a mechanic.
2 The clowns *were* very funny.
3 Her daughter *seems* intelligent.
4 Shakespeare *became* a wealthy man.
5 The farm *appears* profitable.

Each of these verbs tells us something about the subject of the sentence, but it is not an 'action word', it is a 'being word': is, were, seems, became, appears.

REMEMBER

• A verb denotes action or being. Its function in a sentence is to tell us what the subject does or is.

(c) Multiple-word verbs
All the verbs used as examples in Sections 5.3(a) and 5.3(b) consisted of one word, but verbs often consist of more than one word. (See Chapter 12.)

Examples

1 The guests *were told* the news after dinner.
2 We *must leave* next week.
3 That road *has been* dangerous for years.
4 We *shall accept* their offer.
5 I *may go* to the festival.
6 The new valves *will improve* the car's performance.

Sometimes, words that are not part of the verb come between the words that make up the verb.

Examples

1 The weather *has* often *been* cold in May.
2 The scientists *could* not *repeat* the experiment.
3 All the bargains *have* now *vanished* from the shops.
4 You *must* always *try* your best.
5 We *shall*, I am afraid, frequently *be* late on Monday nights.

(d) How to find the verb
1 Find the word (or group of words) that denotes action or being.
2 Check that the word (or group of words) *is* the verb by finding its subject. Since the function of the verb is to tell us what the subject does or is, it follows that a verb must have a subject. Find the subject of the

verb by asking the question *who?* or *what?* before the verb. Whichever word or group of words answers that question is the subject.

Example

Sentence: At the back of the room, near the door, was hanging the famous portrait of Jenny's grandfather.
1 Find the verb – the word or group of words that denotes action or being. In that sentence, the two words *was hanging* form the verb.
2 Check that *was hanging* is the verb by identifying its subject. Ask: *what* 'was hanging'? Answer: 'the famous portrait of Jenny's grandfather was hanging'.
Verb: was hanging
Subject of verb: the famous portrait of Jenny's grandfather

Test 21
Answers on page 163.
Which word or words in each of these sentences tells us what the person or thing named by the subject does or is?

1 Breathless with excitement, Mary untied the parcel.
2 The nocturnal intruder must have opened that window.
3 The ramblers appeared to be very tired.
4 Past midnight, the student was still revising.
5 The rough crossing upset everybody.

Test 22
Answers on page 164.
Identify the subject and the verb in each of these sentences.

Example

The heavy rain of the past week has done a lot of damage.

Subject	Verb
The heavy rain of the past week	has done

1 Have you finished that book?
2 Last year, ten new candidates were accepted for training.
3 Will you be at home on Sunday?
4 A lecturer in engineering should never lack work.
5 We need not keep you any longer.

5.4 PRONOUNS

- A *pronoun* is a word used for/instead of/in place of a noun. The name provides the clue: '*pro*noun'.
- In sentences, pronouns do the same work as nouns. They identify people and things, though they do not specifically name them as do nouns.

Examples

1 George and Hetty had been waiting impatiently for the train and *they* boarded *it* quickly as soon as *it* came in.

they stands for and is used in place of 'George' and 'Hetty'
it stands for and is used in place of 'train'

2 The fugitive tried to dodge the police, but *they* saw *him*.

they stands for and is used in place of 'police'
him stands for and is used in place of 'fugitive'

Often, as in those two sentences, pronouns stand for nouns that have been used previously. A great deal of clumsy repetition would occur if pronouns were not employed.

Example

Peter Jones is playing for the team tomorrow. The selectors have included Peter Jones in the team because the selectors think that Peter Jones will score quickly. The selectors told Peter Jones that Peter Jones had impressed the selectors when Peter Jones played in the trials.

Often, however, the noun for which a pronoun is deputising has not been used already.

Examples

1 *That* is very helpful.

In that sentence, the pronoun *that* refers to something not explicitly named already, but readily identifiable by the speaker/writer or hearer/reader.

2 *These* seem much better value than *those*.

In that sentence, the two pronouns *these* and *those* refer to things not explicitly named. Used in that way, their 'reference' would be indicated by pointing to or looking in the direction of the things that the pronouns signify.

Again, we use pronouns to refer rather generally to persons or things.

Examples

1 *Everything* seemed secure when I left at five o'clock.
2 *Anybody* will tell you how to find the museum.

You will find more information about pronouns in Chapter 12. For the moment, it is sufficient to remember these facts:

(i) Pronouns stand in place of nouns.
(ii) In sentences they do the work of nouns.
(iii) They do *not* describe nouns. That is the job of adjectives – see Section 5.5.

Test 23
Answers on page 164.
Make a list of all the pronouns in this passage.

My name is Robinson. I am the representative for Goldstar Paints. Your next door neighbours have bought several cans and they told me that you might be interested. Everyone speaks highly of Goldstar products. This, for example, is a particularly good outdoor paint. It defeats the worst weather. Everything is protected by a double coat.

5.5 ADJECTIVES

- A word functions as an *adjective* when it tells us more about the person or thing named by a noun or referred to by a pronoun.
- In grammatical terms, the adjective that adds to the meaning of a noun or pronoun is said to *qualify* that noun or pronoun.

Examples

1 The *wealthy* farmer surveyed *his fertile* fields.
2 *Few* prizes were awarded, though *several* candidates excelled.
3 *That* model is a *popular* one, but *those* others are *better*.

Each of the words in italics tells us more about the person or thing named by a noun or referred to by a pronoun. It *qualifies* a noun or a pronoun. It is, therefore, an adjective.

Adjective	Noun or pronoun qualified
wealthy	farmer (noun)
his	fields (noun)
fertile	fields (noun)
few	prizes (noun)
several	candidates (noun)

that	model (noun)
popular	one (pronoun, used in place of noun 'model')
those	others (pronoun, used in place of noun 'models')
better	others (pronoun, used in place of noun 'models')

The adjectives in those sentences add to the meaning of the nouns and pronouns that they qualify in different ways.

Four of the adjectives *describe* the noun or pronoun that they qualify: *wealthy* farmer, *fertile* fields, *popular* one, *better* others. (Although *better* comes after 'others' in the sentence, it still describes that word.)

Two of the adjectives indicate the *number* or *quantity* of the nouns that they qualify: *few* prizes, *several* candidates.

Two of the adjectives *demonstrate* ('point out') the nouns or pronouns that they qualify: *that* model, *those* others.

One of the adjectives indicates the ownership (shows the *possession*) of the noun that it qualifies: *his* fields.

The classification of adjectives is discussed in detail in Chapter 12. For the moment, it is enough to be able to distinguish between adjectives and the other parts of speech.

REMEMBER

- An adjective *always* tells us something more about the person or thing named by a noun or referred to by a pronoun.
- An adjective *always* refers to a particular noun or pronoun present in the sentence. That particular noun or pronoun is said to be *qualified* by the adjective.
- You can be sure that a word is functioning as an adjective when you can identify the particular noun or pronoun that it qualifies.

(a) The position of adjectives functioning as 'describing words'

'Descriptive' adjectives frequently come immediately before the noun or pronoun that they qualify.

Examples

1 My father bought a *large* house.
2 It was not a *happy* place.
3 *Weird* noises disturbed us in the night.
4 At midnight a *terrible* vision appeared.
5 It was the *ghastly* apparition of an *old* man.

A descriptive adjective may be separated from the noun or pronoun that it qualifies. This often happens in sentences in which the verb is a 'being word'.

Examples

1 The weather became *stormy*. (adjective *stormy* qualifies noun 'weather')
2 The harvest was *ripe*. (adjective *ripe* qualifies noun 'harvest')
3 We were *anxious* to start. (adjective *anxious* qualifies pronoun 'we')

(b) The definite and indefinite articles

Although *the* and *a* or *an* function as adjectives, qualifying the nouns that follow them, they are generally referred to as *the definite article* ('the') and *the indefinite article* ('a' or 'an').

Other adjectives often come between the articles and the nouns that they qualify.

Examples

1 The treaty was a botched-up job, doomed to failure
2 An immense but misdirected effort resulted in the ruin of the participants.

(c) Adjectives and pronouns

As you saw in Section 4.2, the same word can have different grammatical functions in different sentences. We have had examples of a word functioning as a 'naming word' - a noun - in one sentence and as an 'action' or 'being word' - a verb - in another.

- We cannot know what part of speech a word is until we see what work it is doing in a sentence.

Bear that fact in mind when classifying a word as either an adjective or a pronoun.

- When a word adds to the meaning of a noun or a pronoun it functions as an *adjective*.
- When a word stands in place of a noun it functions as a *pronoun*.

Examples

Adjectives	Pronouns
I backed *that* horse to win.	*That* was third in the Derby.
Which jockey is best?	Choose *which* you like.
Several writers tipped him.	I shall pick *several*.

Test 24

Answers on page 164.

Identify the adjectives in these sentences, stating the noun or pronoun that each qualifies.

1 Did many people come to see you?
2 This room is too hot.
3 What colour would you like?
4 Use my pen if yours is empty.
5 Their house looks splendid now.
6 Twenty chapters later, that character disappeared from his book.
7 Dwarf tulips grow well in this soil.
8 We must remember to take our fancy dress.
9 Their kind hostess welcomed them with a delicious meal.
10 His record was not broken for ten years.

5.6 ADVERBS

● The name 'adverb' establishes the link between adverbs and verbs. Adverbs add to the meaning of verbs. As we shall see, that is not their only function, but it is a major one.

(a) Adverbs add to the meaning of verbs

Examples

1 Joan's aunt drove *quickly*.

In that sentence, *quickly* functions as an adverb. It adds to the meaning of the verb 'drove' by telling us *how* (the *manner* in which) the action denoted by the verb was performed.
Joan's aunt drove *how?* - quickly.

2 We arrived *early* to avoid the crowds.

In that sentence, *early* functions as an adverb. It adds to the meaning of the verb 'arrived' by telling us *when* the action denoted by the verb was performed.
We arrived *when?* - early.

3 Write your name *there*.

In that sentence, *there* functions as an adverb. It adds to the meaning of the verb 'write' by telling us *where* the action denoted by the verb is to be performed.
Write *where?* - there.

One of the jobs that adverbs often do is to indicate *how*, *when*, or *where* the actions denoted by verbs are performed.
Adverbs also add to the meaning of verbs by telling us *how often* or *to what degree* the actions denoted by verbs are performed.

Examples

1 We called *twice*, but he did not hear us.

In that sentence, *twice* functions as an adverb. It adds to the meaning of the verb 'called' by telling us *how often* the action denoted by the verb was performed.

2 The explorers suffered *much* on the return journey.

In that sentence, *much* functions as an adverb. It adds to the meaning of the verb 'suffered' by telling us *to what degree* (or *to what extent*) the action denoted by the verb was performed.

Adverbs are often used in asking questions. They then indicate that the verb in the question is concerned with:

(i) the *manner* in which the action is performed (*how?*)
(ii) the *time* at which the action is performed (*when?*)
(iii) the *place* at which the action is performed (*where?*)
(iv) the *reason* for which the action is performed (*why?*).

Examples

1 *How* do I find the answer? (*how* adds to the meaning of the verb 'find')
2 *When* will you finish? (*when* adds to the meaning of the verb 'finish')
3 *Where* shall we meet? (*where* adds to the meaning of the verb 'meet')
4 *Why* did they lose that match? (*why* adds to the meaning of the verb 'lose')

In addition to their work as 'verb helpers', adverbs are used to add to the meaning of adjectives and other adverbs.

(b) Adverbs add to the meaning of adjectives

Examples

1 Is this room *too* hot for you?

In that sentence, 'hot' is an adjective qualifying the noun 'room' The word *too* functions as an *adverb*. It adds to the meaning of the adjective 'hot'.

2 The crops were *almost* ripe when the storms began.

In that sentence, 'ripe' is an adjective qualifying the noun 'crops'. The word *almost* functions as an *adverb*. It adds to the meaning of the adjective 'ripe'.

3 He was promoted to a *very* important job.

In that sentence, 'important' is an adjective qualifying the noun 'job'. The word *very* functions as an *adverb*. It adds to the meaning of the adjective 'important'.

(c) Adverbs add to the meaning of other adverbs

Examples

1 The amateur actors spoke *rather* indistinctly.

In that sentence, 'indistinctly' is an adverb adding to the meaning of the verb 'spoke'. The word *rather* also functions as an *adverb*. It adds to the meaning of the adverb 'indistinctly'.

2 He arrived *too* late to see the first act.

In that sentence, 'late' is an adverb adding to the meaning of the verb 'arrived'. The word *too* also functions as an *adverb*. It adds to the meaning of the adverb 'late'.

3 She paints *extremely* well.

In that sentence, 'well' is an adverb adding to the meaning of the verb 'paints'. The word *extremely* also functions as an *adverb*. It adds to the meaning of the adverb 'well'.

We can now complete our definition of the term *adverb*.

● An adverb is a word that adds to the meaning of a verb, an adjective or another adverb.

(d) The grammatical terms 'qualify' and 'modify'

As we saw in Section 5.5, adjectives add to the meaning of nouns and pronouns. In grammatical terms, *adjectives* are said to *qualify* nouns and pronouns.

In this section, we have seen that adverbs add to the meaning of verbs, adjectives and other adverbs. In grammatical terms, *adverbs* are said to *modify* verbs, adjectives, and other adverbs.

Some writers on grammar think that the distinction between the terms *qualify* and *modify* is not important. Since both adjectives and adverbs function by adding to the meaning of other words, they argue that one term is sufficient, and they use the term *modify* to describe the work of both adjectives and adverbs.

Nevertheless, the distinction between *qualify* (adjectives qualify) and *modify* (adverbs modify) is widely maintained. It will be adhered to in this book so that you will not be confused when you encounter the two terms elsewhere.

(e) Adjectives and adverbs

An understanding of the fundamental difference between the function of adjectives and the function of adverbs is much more important than the argument about 'qualify' and 'modify'.

Both parts of speech add to the meaning of other words, but

REMEMBER

- Adjectives add to the meaning of nouns and pronouns. Adverbs do *not*.
- Adverbs add to the meaning of verbs, adjectives and adverbs. Adjectives do *not*.

A graphic representation helps to press home this all-important point:

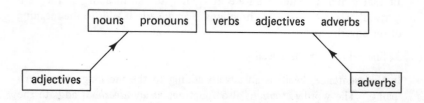

(f) Is it an adjective or an adverb?

REMEMBER

- A word *is* what it *does* in a sentence.

By now, you are familiar with the way in which a word can change its grammatical function from one sentence to another.

Examples

1 These are the oldest *rocks* known to man. (*rocks* is a noun)
2 Their immense age *rocks* our imagination. (*rocks* is a verb)
3 Do you believe *that*? (*that* is a pronoun)
4 Yes, if *that* man says it is true. (*that* is an adjective)

So, too, the *same* word can function as an *adjective* in one sentence and as an *adverb* in another.

Examples

1 They arrived at the theatre *late*.

In that sentence, *late* is an *adverb* because it adds to the meaning of (modifies) the verb 'arrived'.

2 Their *late* arrival disturbed the audience.

In that sentence, *late* is an *adjective* because it adds to the meaning of (qualifies) the noun 'arrival'.

3 Accounts are rendered *weekly*.

In that sentence, *weekly* is an *adverb* because it adds to the meaning of (modifies) the verb 'are rendered'.

4 *Weekly* accounts are rendered.

In that sentence, *weekly* is an *adjective* because it adds to the meaning of (qualifies) the noun 'accounts'.

Test 25
Answers on page 164.
Identify the adverbs in these sentences and name the verb, adjective, or adverb modified by each.

1 Did you have to wait long?
2 We had exceptionally good audiences for that film.
3 She answered rather unwillingly.
4 Where are you going for your holidays?
5 The balloon rose very slowly.
6 Keep your head down.
7 Why can't they agree amicably?
8 The defeated candidate said little, but she suffered much.
9 Get well quickly.
10 The years go by so fast.

Test 26
Answers on page 164.
Which of the italicised words are adjectives and which are adverbs? Give reasons for your answers.

1 The favourite came *last* in the three o'clock race.
2 The favourite was the *last* horse in the three o'clock race.
3 This is an *easy* test.
4 The candidate felt *easy*.
5 By morning, the winds were *still*.
6 The pilot is *still* trying to land.
7 She, *too*, is eligible for a grant.
8 Bring your sister *too*.
9 The office workers collected their pay *monthly*.
10 A *monthly* cheque is very comforting.

5.7 PREPOSITIONS

(a) Definition
A *preposition* is the first word of a *phrase* that contains a *noun* or a *pronoun*. A phrase of this kind *does the work of an adjective or an adverb*.

Examples

The prepositions are printed in capitals and the phrases are underlined.

1 The car IN the garage had a flat battery.
2 The river flowed UNDER a bridge.
3 AFTER the party we did a lot of washing-up.
4 The bad-tempered man replied WITH a grunt.
5 The repairs TO the roof were completed quickly.
6 She reached the house BEFORE me.

(b) Prepositional phrase = preposition + noun or pronoun
The name *preposition* means 'placed before'. A preposition is placed before a noun or a pronoun to make a prepositional phrase.

Examples

1 in the garage	preposition IN + noun *garage*	
2 under the bridge	preposition UNDER + noun *bridge*	
3 after the party	preposition AFTER + noun *party*	
4 with a grunt	preposition WITH + noun *grunt*	
5 to the roof	preposition TO + noun *roof*	
6 before me	preposition BEFORE + pronoun *me*	

REMEMBER

● Every prepositional phrase consists of a preposition plus a noun or a pronoun.

(c) Prepositional phrases function as adjectives or as adverbs
As we saw in Section 2.2, a phrase is a group of words that does *not* make complete sense *on its own*. When it is used as part of a sentence, however, it adds to the meaning of that sentence.

A prepositional phrase does not make complete sense on its own, but it enlarges the meaning of a sentence by telling us more about *a particular word* in that sentence.

Examples

Sentence	Sentence + prepositional phrase
1 The car had a flat battery.	The car *in the garage* had a flat battery.
2 The river flowed.	The river flowed *under a bridge.*

In 1 the prepositional phrase *in the garage* tells us more about the thing named by the noun 'car' Therefore the prepositional phrase functions as an *adjective*. It qualifies the noun 'car'.

In 2 the prepositional phrase *under the bridge* tells us more about the action denoted by the verb 'flowed'. Therefore the prepositional phrase functions as an *adverb*. It modifies the verb 'flowed'.

Look at the other examples in Section 5.7(a) and you will see that each prepositional phrase functions in its sentence as either an adjective or an adverb.

3 prepositional phrase *after the party* is an adverb-phrase modifying verb 'did'

4 prepositional phrase *with a grunt* is an adverb-phrase modifying verb 'replied'

5 prepositional phrase *to the roof* is an adjective-phrase qualifying noun 'repairs'

6 prepositional phrase *before me* is an adverb-phrase modifying verb 'reached'

(d) The preposition as a 'relating' word
The preposition indicates a relationship (makes a connection) between the noun or pronoun that follows it in the phrase and another word in the sentence. Like this:
1 The repairs to the roof were completed quickly.

preposition *to* indicates a relationship between 'roof' (the noun in the phrase) and 'repairs', a noun elsewhere in the sentence: the preposition connects them

2 The river flowed under the bridge.

preposition *under* indicates a relationship between 'bridge' (the noun in the phrase) and 'flowed', a verb elsewhere in the sentence: the preposition connects them

REMEMBER

● A preposition relates the noun or pronoun in the prepositional phrase to another word elsewhere in the sentence. That other word is: a noun *or* a pronoun *or* a verb *or* an adjective.

Examples

1 The coach for London leaves from this bay.

preposition *for* relates noun 'London' to noun 'coach'

phrase *for London* is an adjective-phrase qualifying noun 'coach'
preposition *from* relates noun 'bay' to verb 'leaves'
phrase *from this bay* is an adverb-phrase modifying verb 'leaves'

2 Those in the basket look fresh.

preposition *in* relates noun 'basket' to pronoun 'those'
phrase *in the basket* is an adjective-phrase qualifying pronoun 'those'

3 I shall divide the money between them.

preposition *between* relates pronoun 'them' to verb 'shall divide'
phrase *between them* is an adverb-phrase modifying verb 'shall divide'

4 The actor's eyes were full of tears.

preposition *of* relates noun 'tears' to adjective 'full'
phrase *of tears* is an adverb-phrase modifying adjective 'full'

(e) Compound prepositions
A preposition sometimes consists of more than one word.

Examples

1 The land was farmed *in accordance with* the best modern ideas.
2 *With regard to* the law, I find nothing to prohibit this action.
3 The ministers resigned *because of* their defeat.

(f) Preposition or adverb?

REMEMBER

• A word is classified as a particular part of speech according to the work that it is doing in a particular sentence.

The following words are often used as prepositions, but they can also be used as adverbs: at, after, above, along, across, around, by, before, below, beneath, down, for, from, in, near, on, to, through, under, with.

Examples

1 Come *across* now.
adverb *across* modifies verb 'come'

2 Come *across* the road now.
preposition *across* is the first word of the adverb-phrase *across the road* modifying verb 'come'

3 Can you see *down*?
adverb *down* modifies verb 'see'

4 Can you see *down* the well?
preposition *down* is the first word of the adverb-phrase *down the well* modifying verb 'see'

REMEMBER

- A preposition is *always* followed by a noun or a pronoun which completes the phrase introduced by the preposition. The preposition cannot be split away from the rest of the phrase.

Test 27
Answers on page 165.
Identify the prepositions in these sentences. Write out each prepositional phrase in full and describe its function in the sentence.

Example

These flowers are lovely, but those in the centre are fading.

Preposition	Prepositional phrase	Function
in	in the centre	adjective-phrase qualifying pronoun 'those'

 1 The treasure was buried underneath the grey stone.
 2 I am happy with your decision.
 3 The house was a heap of rubble.
 4 Candidates from that school always do well.
 5 They are proud of their football team.
 6 Answers – on a postcard – should reach us by Monday.
 7 The news was broadcast at six o'clock.
 8 The champion withdrew from the final because of his injury.
 9 A minor official was sent in place of the minister.
10 Nothing grows in that poor soil.

5.8 CONJUNCTIONS

As the name *con-junction* suggests, a conjunction is a word used to *join together* or *connect* words or groups of words.

Examples

1 Fish *and* chips follow the Englishman round the world.
conjunction *and* joins the two nouns 'fish' 'chips'

2 The tourists arrived by road *and* by rail.
conjunction *and* joins the two phrases 'by road' 'by rail'

3 My dog is small *but* ferocious.
conjunction *but* joins the two adjectives 'small' 'ferocious'

4 The giant was ugly *but* he was kind.
conjunction *but* joins two sentences 'The giant was ugly' 'he was kind'.
The use of a conjunction here turns two separate sentences into a *double*
sentence (see Section 9.4).

5 Her opponents regarded her without respect *but* without malice.
conjunction *but* joins the two phrases 'without respect' 'without malice'

Conjunctions often work in pairs.

Examples

1 The happy man is *neither* poor *nor* wealthy.
paired conjunctions *neither/nor* join adjectives 'poor' and 'wealthy'

2 He must have been *either* clever *or* fortunate.
paired conjunctions *either/or* join adjectives 'clever' and 'fortunate'

REMEMBER

- All the conjunctions used in those examples are *co-ordinating conjunctions*. That is, they join words or groups of words that play similar
  parts in the sentence.

Later in this book you will learn about conjunctions that join words or
groups of words that play different parts in the sentence.

5.9 INTERJECTIONS

Useful though they are, interjections play no part in the grammar of a
sentence.
    Interjections are words (or representations of sounds) 'thrown in'
(*inter-jected*) to express feelings or attitudes. When written, an interjection
is often followed immediately by an exclamation mark.

Examples

Oh! you can't be serious.
Mm! I thought so.

Often, however, a comma follows the interjection, and the exclamation
mark is held back to the end of the sentence, or omitted.

Oh, you can't be serious!
Mm, I thought so.

The punctuation indicates whether the emphasis is placed on the interjection or on the sentence.

Sometimes, an interjection consists of a phrase, or even a sentence.

Examples

1 *What a shame*, he's failed!
2 *Thank goodness*, there's a vacancy.
3 *I say*, have you heard the news?

When such a sentence is analysed, however, the interjection is ignored, for it has no grammatical function.

Example

Really, I am amazed!

The subject is 'I' and the predicate is 'am amazed'. The interjection 'Really' plays no part in either.

5.10 FAMILY GROUPS AND WORD BEHAVIOUR

A useful way of remembering the names of the eight parts of speech is to think of them in 'family groups'.

Family 1	Family 2	Family 3	'Orphans'
nouns	verbs	prepositions	interjections
pronouns	adverbs	conjunctions	
adjectives			

Of course, the members of those 'word families' do not keep themselves to themselves in stand-offish isolation. In the busy world of the sentence, the parts of speech work together, forming alliances according to the laws of English grammar.

Nouns and pronouns team up with verbs to form subjects and predicates. Adjectives link hands with nouns and pronouns. Adverbs consort with verbs, adjectives, and other adverbs. Prepositions relate with nouns, pronouns, verbs and adjectives. Conjunctions join words and groups of words together.

Finally, as we have seen, individual words often change their family group from one sentence to another, functioning – for example – as a noun in this sentence, a verb in that; a pronoun in this, an adjective in that; a preposition in this, an adverb in that.

● It is the work that a word does *in a sentence* that determines what part of speech it is.

THE PARTS OF THE SIMPLE SENTENCE

6.1 DEFINITION OF THE SIMPLE SENTENCE

As we have seen earlier:

(i) Every sentence consists of a subject and a predicate.
(ii) Every predicate must contain a verb.

It follows that every sentence must contain a verb and the subject of that verb.

A *simple sentence* contains *one* verb (and *only* one verb) plus the subject of that verb.

Not all sentences are simple, of course. Many have more than one verb and more than one subject. Nevertheless, the grammar of the simple sentence lays down the basic pattern on which all other sentences are built.

REMEMBER

● When applied to a sentence, the term 'simple' has nothing to do with its length (long or short) or its content (intellectually easy or difficult). 'Simple' has a precise grammatical meaning. It denotes a sentence that contains *one* verb and the *subject* of that verb.

Examples

1 Fish swim.

A *simple* sentence. It contains *one verb* ('swim') and the *subject* of that verb ('fish').

2 A week or so back, our local auctioneers sent me catalogues of all their forthcoming sales for the rest of this year.

A *simple* sentence. It contains *one verb* ('sent') and the *subject* of that verb ('our local auctioneers').

6.2 SUBJECT AND PREDICATE

These are the two fundamental parts of the simple sentence. The subject names the person, thing or idea about which something is being said. The predicate tells us something about the person, thing or idea named by the subject.

Use this method when analysing a simple sentence into subject and predicate:

1 *Find the verb.* The verb is an 'action word' or a 'being word'. It may consist of more than one word, but multi-word verbs, like single-word verbs, denote action or being.

2 *Check that it is the verb by finding its subject.* Put the question *who?* or *what?* before the verb. The word or words that answer that question are the subject of the verb.

3 *Take out the subject*, and all the other words (*including* the verb) are the predicate.

Example

After Brown's sudden departure, Smith made a terrible mess of the paperwork in the department.

1 *Find the verb.* The verb is the 'action word' *made*.

2 *Find the subject.* Ask 'who made?' or 'what made?'. The answer is: 'Smith made'. The subject is *Smith*.

3 *Take out the subject.* All the words that remain form the predicate.

6.3 THE SUBJECT AND THE SUBJECT-WORD

When the subject of a sentence consists of more than one word, the sense of the sentence tells us that *one* of the words forming the subject is more closely linked with the verb than any of the others.

That word is the *subject-word*. It is the most important word in the subject. If it is omitted, the link between the subject and the verb is snapped.

Examples

1 His heavy *boots* blistered his feet.
2 The cunning old *fox* escaped.
3 Her tired *eyes* made her head ache.

Subject	Subject-word	Verb
1 his heavy boots	boots	blistered
2 the cunning old fox	fox	escaped
3 her tired eyes	eyes	made

- There can be no subject (and, therefore, no sentence) without a subject-word.

Examples

1 his heavy – blistered his feet
2 the cunning old – escaped
3 her tired – made her head ache

There may be more than one subject-word in a sentence.

Examples

1 My *parents* and *I* were on holiday.
2 *Smith, Brown* and *Jones* lost marks in the oral test.
3 *Oats* and *barley* grow on that farm.

In a *simple* sentence, however, there is only *one verb*. The two subject-words, 'parents' and 'I' in sentence 1 are both linked to the *one* verb: *were*. There is only *one verb* in each of the other sentences also: *lost* in sentence 2 and *grow* in sentence 3.

6.4 SUBJECT-WORD AND WORDS QUALIFYING SUBJECT-WORD

Since the function of the subject is to name the person, thing or idea about which the predicate tells us something, it follows that the subject-word must always be a noun or a pronoun – a 'naming word'.

The words that make up the rest of the subject tell us more about the subject-word. That is to say, they function as *adjectives* qualifying the subject-word.

Examples

1 The noisy spectators upset the speaker.
2 A woman in a blue coat barracked continuously.
3 The angry stewards removed her and her friends.

Subject-word	Adjectives or adjective-phrases qualifying subject-word	
1 spectators	the	noisy
2 woman	a	in a blue coat
3 stewards	the	angry

Notice that the definite and indefinite articles are included with the other qualifying words since they function as adjectives.

We can now analyse those three examples in some detail and set the results out in a convenient tabular form.

Subject		Predicate	
subject-word	*adjectives or adjective-phrases*	*verb*	*rest of predicate*
1 spectators	the noisy	upset	the speaker
2 woman	a in a blue coat	barracked	continuously
3 stewards	the angry	removed	her and her friends

Test 28
Answers on page 166.
Analyse these sentences. Set your results out in a table as shown above.

1 The last train leaves at midnight.
2 A revolver with a pearl handle provided a vital clue.
3 Those books on that shelf in the library are not often read.
4 In the background I could see several familiar faces.
5 Use that big spanner.

6.5 PREDICATE: THE VERB AND WORDS MODIFYING THE VERB

As we saw in Section 5.3, the verb is the most important word in the predicate. Its function is to tell us something about the subject. Therefore, a predicate may consist solely of that one part of speech: the verb.

Nevertheless, a predicate usually contains other words in addition to the verb. To understand the grammar of the predicate, we have to understand the function of those other words.

Words in the predicate may tell us something more about the verb. That is, they function as *adverbs* modifying the verb.

Examples

1 The tired climbers advanced *slowly*.
2 They moved *with great effort*.
3 *From the base camp* we watched *through our glasses*.

A tabular analysis makes clear the adverbial function of the italicised words in those examples.

Subject		Predicate	
subject-word	adjectives or adjective-phrases	verb	adverbs or adverb-phrases
1 climbers	the tired	advanced	slowly
2 they		moved	with great effort
3 we		watched	from the base camp through our glasses

6.6 PREDICATE: THE DIRECT OBJECT

A verb denoting *action* may be followed by a *direct object*. Such a verb is called a *transitive verb*.

REMEMBER

The meaning of *trans-* is 'across' (as in *transatlantic*). A verb with a direct object is called a transitive verb because the action of the verb is 'carried across' to the direct object.

Examples

1 We sang *songs*.
2 I was eating *sweets*.
3 Columbus discovered *America*.
4 Cats catch *mice*.
5 The children stole *apples*.
6 Wellington defeated *Napoleon*.

The italicised word in each of those sentences is the *direct object* of the verb. The action denoted by the verb is 'carried across' to the person or thing named by the direct object.

Ask the question *what?* or *whom?* after the verb. The word that gives the answer to the question is the direct object.

Examples

We sang songs.

We sang *what?*: songs – so *songs* is the direct object of the verb 'sang'

Wellington defeated Napoleon.

Wellington defeated *whom?*: Napoleon – so *Napoleon* is the direct object of the verb 'defeated'

A verb denoting action is not necessarily followed by a direct object.

Examples

1 We sang songs./We sang.
2 I was eating sweets./I was eating.
3 The children stole apples./The children stole.

REMEMBER

- A verb denoting action and having a direct object is a *transitive* verb.
- A verb denoting action and *not* having a direct object is an *intransitive* verb.
- The *same* verb can be used transitively or intransitively. See the examples just given.

The *direct object* is that part of the predicate that names the person or thing on which the action denoted by the verb is performed. The action is 'carried across to' the direct object. The direct object 'suffers' the action denoted by the verb. All those descriptions are used to describe the relationship between a verb and its direct object.

It is clear that *only* a verb denoting action can have a direct object. A verb denoting being (for example: 'is', 'seem', 'become') cannot have a direct object, for there is no action to be 'carried across'.

Notice, too, that a sentence containing a direct object can be reversed, so that the direct object becomes the subject *without changing the sense of the sentence.*

Examples

1 The policeman chased the thief./The thief was chased by the policeman.
2 The delighted winner claimed the huge prize./The huge prize was claimed by the delighted winner.

REMEMBER

- The direct object *names* the person or thing that 'suffers' the action of the verb.
- Therefore, the direct object-word must be a *noun* or a *pronoun.*
- It follows, too, that the direct object-word may be *qualified* by other words. Those other words must, then, be adjectives or adjective-phrases.

Example

The firm is recruiting suitable candidates in the right age group.

The firm is recruiting *what?*: suitable candidates in the right age group.
Direct object: suitable candidates in the right age group
Direct object-word: candidates
Adjectives or adjective-phrases qualifying direct object-word: suitable; in the right age-group.

Test 29
Answers on page 166.
Identify the direct object-words and any qualifying words. **Note** Not all
the sentences contain direct objects.

1 Hamlet killed Polonius.
2 The children explored the deserted island.
3 My aunt sighed every now and then.
4 They could see another shore across the water.
5 The worshippers veiled their eyes.
6 Peter had learnt a hard lesson.
7 The doors banged all night in the haunted house.
8 We screamed with terror.
9 The procession marched in dignified silence.
10 The champion won every round.

Test 30
Answers on page 167.
Analyse these sentences, using this table.

Subject		Predicate			
subject-word	adjectives or adjective-phrases	verb	adverbs or adverb-phrases	direct object-word	adjectives or adjective-phrases

1 Old pictures often make big prices at auctions.
2 This grim prison held many unfortunate captives in the early eighteenth
century.
3 Space yields its secrets slowly.

6.7 PREDICATE: THE INDIRECT OBJECT

A verb denoting action may be followed by an *indirect object*.

Examples

1 Kate gave Jean an expensive present.

Kate gave *what?* – an expensive present (*direct object*)
Kate gave an expensive present *to whom?* – Jean (*indirect object*)

2 The appeal court granted the defendant a retrial.

The appeal court granted *what?* – a retrial (*direct object*)
The appeal court granted a retrial *to whom?* – the defendant (*indirect
object*)

3 The chef made the late arrivals a hasty supper.

The chef made *what?* – a hasty supper (*direct object*)
The chef made a hasty supper *for whom?* – the late arrivals (*indirect object*)

REMEMBER

● The *indirect object* is that part of the predicate that names the person or thing *affected by* the action denoted by the verb – the person or thing *to whom* or *for whom* the action is done.
● Therefore, the indirect object can be replaced by a phrase beginning with *to* or *for*.

Examples

1 I gave *Jack* a camera./I gave a camera *to Jack.*
2 They offered *him* a job./They offered a job *to him.*
3 She made *me* tea./She made tea *for me.*

Note that the prepositional phrases 'to Jack', 'to him', 'for me' are adverb-phrases modifying the verbs 'gave', 'offered', 'made'.

REMEMBER

● Like the subject-word and the direct object-word, the indirect object-word must be a noun or a pronoun, and it may, therefore, be qualified by adjectives or adjective-phrases.

Example

The optimistic travellers showed the baffled inspector their out-of-date tickets.

Subject-word: travellers
Words qualifying subject-word: the   optimistic
Direct object-word: tickets
Words qualifying direct object-word: their   out-of-date
Indirect object-word: inspector
Words qualifying indirect object-word: the   baffled

Test 31
Answers on page 167.
Find the indirect object in each of these sentences.

1 In his will he is leaving the institute a large sum of money.
2 The benevolent champion gave the sports club all his trophies.
3 The lecturer showed the audience a new set of slides.

4 We offered the greedy vendor half his price.
5 Please cut me a ham sandwich.

6.8 PREDICATE: PREDICATIVE WORDS (OR COMPLEMENT)

(a) Predicative words and 'being' verbs

As we saw in Section 6.6, a verb denoting action may be used *transitively*, with a direct object to which its action is 'carried across'.('The choir sang an anthem'.)

We also saw that a verb denoting action may be used *intransitively*, without a direct object and forming a predicate on its own. ('The choir sang'.)

We saw, too, that a verb denoting being *cannot* have a direct object, since there is no action to be 'carried across'.

There is yet another way in which verbs denoting being behave differently from verbs denoting action:

● A verb denoting being cannot form a predicate *on its own*. It requires the help of additional words to complete the sense of its predicate.

Examples

1 Jones is. . .   (is what?)
2 Richard became. . .   (became what?)
3 That girl seems. . .   (seems what?)

Additional words must be supplied to complete those predicates:

1 Jones is *a grocer*.
2 Richard became *serious*.
3 That girl seems *intelligent*.

Those additional words *a grocer*, *serious*, *intelligent* are 'predicative words', completing the predicates of the being verbs 'is', 'became' and 'seems'.

● The word or words that complete the predicate of a verb denoting being are called *predicative words*.

Predicative words may be nouns or pronouns or adjectives. Predicative nouns or pronouns may be qualified by adjectives or adjective-phrases. Predicative adjectives may be modified by adverbs or adverb-phrases.

When predicative words complete the predicate of a verb denoting being, they refer to the same person, thing or idea as is named by the subject of the verb.

Examples

1 My brother is AN ATHLETE *of considerable promise*.
[AN] ATHLETE: predicative noun completing predicate of being verb 'is'

and referring to the subject of that verb: 'My brother'
of considerable promise: adjective-phrase qualifying predicative noun 'athlete'

2 Joan was *very* VIVACIOUS.

VIVACIOUS: predicative adjective completing predicate of being verb 'was' and referring to the subject of that verb: 'Joan'
very: adverb modifying predicative adjective 'vivacious'.

3 After the merger, the two companies became ONE *of the market leaders.*

ONE: predicative pronoun completing predicate of being verb 'became' and referring to the subject of that verb: 'the two companies'
of the market leaders: adjective-phrase qualifying predicative pronoun: 'one'

You will not be in any danger of confusing direct objects and predicative words if you:

REMEMBER

- A 'being' verb *cannot* have a direct object.
- A direct object *never* refers to the same person, thing or idea as that named by the subject.
- Predicative words completing the predicate of a 'being' verb *always* refer to the same person, thing or idea as that named by the subject.

Examples

1 My brother is an *athlete*. (predicative noun completing sense of being verb 'is' and referring to the same person as is named by the subject-word 'brother')
2 My brother coached an *athlete*. (direct object of action verb 'coached' and does *not* refer to the same person as is named by the subject-word 'brother')

(b) Predicative words and 'action verbs'
Sometimes the direct object of an action verb requires additional words to complete its meaning.

Examples

1 The news of victory made him *happy*.
2 The racing driver called that doll *his talisman*.
3 The members elected Hilda Brown *chairperson*.

In such sentences, the predicative words complete the meaning of the direct object. Unlike predicative words following a being verb, they refer to the object *not* to the subject. For this reason, they are often described as the 'objective complement'.

The grammatical term *complement* is often used as a synonym for the term 'predicative words'. It is a reminder that the function of predicative words is:

(i) to *complete* the predicate of a being verb;
(ii) to *complete* the direct object of some action verbs.

Test 32
Answers on page 167.
Describe the functions of the italicised words and phrases in these sentences.

1 He became *notorious for his crimes*.
2 The old man always appeared *contented*.
3 Those sweets are not *good for you*.
4 That empty house looks *very sinister*.
5 Shall I seem *greedy*?

Test 33
Answers on page 167.
Make an analysis of the *predicate* of each of these sentences, using these headings.

Verb	Adverbs or adverb-phrases modifying verb	Direct object-word	Adjectives or adjective-phrases qualifying direct object-word	Indirect object-word	Adjectives or adjective-phrases qualifying indirect object-word	Predicative word + words qualifying or modifying predicative word

Do not expect to find *all* those parts in *every* predicate.

1 The dying swan sang its melancholy song.
2 Is this a cure for indigestion?
3 Did he invent a cure for indigestion?
4 The failure of the harvest in the eastern provinces caused the worst famine in the history of that country.
5 At nine o'clock I finished the novel.
6 In the night, the compassionate guard gave the wakeful prisoner a drink from his flask.

6.9 A TABULAR LIST OF ALL THE PARTS OF THE SIMPLE SENTENCE

Having now discussed each of the parts that a simple sentence may contain, we can list them in a table.

Subject		Predicate						
subject-word	adjectives or adjective-phrases qualifying subject-word	verb	adverbs or adverb-phrases modifying verb	direct object-word	adjectives or adjective-phrases qualifying direct object-word	indirect object-word	adjectives or adjective-phrases qualifying indirect object-word	predicative word + words qualifying or modifying predicative word

Every simple sentence *must* contain two of those parts: the subject-word and the verb. In addition, it *may* contain all or some of the other parts.

FINITE VERBS AND NON-FINITE VERBS

In Chapters 5 and 6 we studied the work that words do in simple sentences, learning how to identify a word as a particular part of speech by recognising its function in a sentence.

We cannot make a full analysis of the simple sentence, however, until we understand an aspect of verb behaviour that we have not yet discussed. We know already that the verb in a simple sentence must have a subject, but we have not yet studied the verb without a subject.

A verb without a subject (a *non-finite verb*, as it is called) often plays an important part in the grammar of a simple sentence.

REMEMBER

- There is *always* a verb *with* a subject (a *finite* verb) in a simple sentence.
- A verb *without* a subject (a *non-finite* verb) *may also* be present in a simple sentence.

7.1 FINITE VERBS

In Section 6.1, a simple sentence was defined as a sentence containing *one* verb and the *subject* of that verb. Here is another way of wording that definition:

- A simple sentence is a sentence containing one (and only one) *finite* verb.

To which we can now add this further definition:

- A *finite* verb is a verb that has a *subject*.

(a) The meaning of the term 'finite verb'

The word *finite* means 'limited'. In general speech, the opposite of *finite* is 'infinite'. We say, for example, that an individual human life is finite, whereas eternity is infinite.

In grammar, we use the term *finite verb* to describe a verb that is 'limited' and we use the term *non-finite verb* to describe a verb that is 'not limited'.

(b) A verb is 'limited' by having a subject

When a verb has a subject, it is 'pinned down' – *limited* – by that subject.

Examples

1a   He *runs* quickly.
1b   I *run* quickly.
2a   The shops *stay* open late.
2b   The shop *stays* open late.

The verb-forms in those examples are fixed – *limited* – by their respective subject-words. In 1a the subject-word 'He' requires the verb-form *runs*. It will not accept the verb-form *run*. In 2a the subject-word 'shops' requires the verb-form *stay*. It will not accept the verb-form *stays*.

REMEMBER

• A finite verb is limited by its subject-word. It takes the verb-form that its subject-word requires.

(c) A finite verb is limited in 'number' and in 'person'

In grammatical terms, we say that a finite verb 'agrees with' its subject-word in 'number' and in 'person'.

You will find further information about number and person in Chapter 12. Here we shall consider those two terms only in so far as we need their help in understanding the difference between finite verbs and non-finite verbs.

NUMBER   There are two numbers: singular (one) and plural (more than one). According to its subject-word, a finite verb must be either singular or plural. When its subject-word is singular, the verb must be singular. When its subject-word is plural, the verb must be plural.

PERSON   There are three persons: 1st, 2nd and 3rd. Each person may be either singular or plural. The verb must be the same person as its subject-word.

REMEMBER

• Every finite verb – according to its subject-word – must be singular or plural and it must be 1st or 2nd or 3rd person.

Examples

1 I arrive. (verb is 1st person singular)
2 You arrive. (verb is 2nd person singular)
3 He/She/It arrives. (verb is 3rd person singular)
4 We arrive. (verb is 1st person plural)
5 You arrive. (verb is 2nd person plural)
6 They arrive. (verb is 3rd person plural)
7 The train (*it*) arrives. (verb is 3rd person singular)
8 The trains (*they*) arrive. (verb is 3rd person plural)

As Examples 7 and 8 show, when the subject-word is a noun, the person and number of the verb can be discovered by substituting the appropriate pronoun for the noun.

Examples

1 The driver (*he* or *she*) swerved. (verb is 3rd person singular)
2 The car (*it*) swerved. (verb is 3rd person singular)
3 The cars (*they*) swerved. (verb is 3rd person plural)

In fact, when the subject-word is a noun, the verb *must* be in the 3rd person, but it may be either singular or plural according to the number of its subject-word.

(d) A finite verb is limited by tense
'Tense' means 'time'. Every verb with a subject denotes action or being that exists in time, either in the past, in the present or in the future.

Examples

1 The car *ran* smoothly. (verb is in past tense)
2 The car *runs* smoothly. (verb is in present tense)
3 The car *will run* smoothly. (verb is in future tense)

The tenses of verbs are explained in Chapter 12. For the moment, the distinction between past, present and future tenses is all we need consider.

To sum up:

● A verb with a subject is a finite verb, limited by having a particular number, person, and tense.

7.2 NON-FINITE VERBS

As we have said, a sentence *must* contain a verb with a subject (a finite verb); and it *may* also contain a verb without a subject (a non-finite verb).

Examples
The finite verbs are printed in capitals. The non-finite verbs are printed in italics.

1 *Hoping* for good news, we TELEPHONED the hospital.
2 She EXPECTS *to pass* her test.
3 The mechanics STARTED *repairing* the engine.
4 *Distracted* by the noise, our driver TOOK the wrong road.
5 *Sewing* IS an extremely important skill.

As those examples show, each finite verb denotes action or being and it has a subject-word. Each non-finite verb denotes action or being but it has not got a subject-word.

There are four kinds of non-finite verbs: 1 the infinitive, 2 the gerund; 3 the present participle; 4 the past participle.

Full information about the non-finite forms of the verb is provided in Chapter 12. Here, we are concerned only with their special functions as parts of the simple sentence.

(a) The infinitive
The infinitive usually begins with the preposition *to* ('to walk', 'to see', 'to be', and so on). It is the *name* of the verb. In a sentence it has three functions: it acts as a verb-noun *or* as a verb-adverb *or* as a verb-adjective.

(i) The infinitive functioning as a verb-noun

Examples

1 *To walk* is healthy.

The infinitive is the subject of the verb 'is'. It therefore functions as a noun, but it also functions as a verb because it denotes action.

2 *To win* that match was his greatest ambition.

The infinitive is the subject of the verb 'was'. It therefore functions as a noun, but it also functions as a verb because it denotes action and it has a direct object of its own: 'that match'.

3 We tried *to open* the window.

The infinitive is the direct object of the verb 'tried'. It therefore functions as a noun, but it also functions as a verb because it denotes action and it has a direct object of its own: 'the window'.

4 Her aim is *to become* a doctor.

The infinitive functions as a predicative noun completing the predicate of the verb 'is'. It also functions as a verb because it denotes being and it has a predicative noun of its own: 'doctor'.

(ii) The infinitive functions as a verb-adverb

Examples

1 The tourists come *to enjoy* our scenery.

The infinitive functions as an adverb modifying the verb 'come'. It also functions as a verb because it denotes action and it has a direct object: 'our scenery'.

2 She is too hot-tempered *to be* reliable.

The infinitive functions as an adverb modifying the adjective 'hot-tempered'. It also functions as a verb because it denotes being and it has a complement of its own: 'reliable'.

(iii) The infinitive functions as a verb-adjective

Examples

1 The tourists have plenty of money *to spend* in the shops.

The infinitive functions as an adjective qualifying the noun 'money'. It also functions as a verb because it denotes action and it is modified by an adverb-phrase: 'in the shops'.

2 Is there anything *to eat* on the train?

The infinitive functions as an adjective qualifying the pronoun 'anything'. It also functions as a verb because it denotes action and it is modified by the adverb-phrase: 'on the train'.

(b) The gerund
The gerund is a verb-form ending in *-ing* ('walking', 'talking', 'laughing', and so on). It *always* functions as a *verb-noun*.

Examples

1 *Rolling* the lawn is hard work

The gerund is the subject-word of the verb 'is'. It therefore functions as a noun, but it also functions as a verb because it denotes action and it has a direct object: 'the lawn'.

2 They have begun *repairing* the car.

The gerund is the direct object of the verb 'have begun'. It therefore functions as a noun, but it also functions as a verb because it denotes action and it has a direct object of its own: 'the car'.

3 A gardener's most frequent task is *weeding*.

The gerund functions as a predicative noun completing the predicate of the verb 'is'.

4 The star upset her manager by *cancelling* her contract.

'Be off!'
an angry gerund will have nothing to do with present participles

The gerund functions as a noun in the prepositional phrase: 'by *cancelling* her contract'. That prepositional phrase is an adverb-phrase modifying the verb 'upset'. The gerund also functions as a verb because it denotes action and it has a direct object: 'her contract'.

REMEMBER

- A gerund is a verb-form ending in *-ing*. In a simple sentence, it performs the function of a noun by acting as subject-word, object-word, predicative noun or by following a preposition in a prepositional phrase.

The gerund may be qualified by an adjective preceded by either the definite or the indefinite article: 'The discordant *braying* of the trumpets broke the peace of the afternoon'. In such examples, the noun function of the gerund is so dominant that it may be described simply as a noun.

(c) The present participle

Like the gerund, the present participle is a verb-form ending in *-ing* ('worrying', 'passing', 'urging', and so on); *but* whereas the gerund is a verb-noun, the present participle is a *verb-adjective*.

Examples

1 His illness gave us all a *worrying* time.
2 The noise of the *passing* traffic interrupted our conversation.
3 Their report was very *depressing.*

'People forget that I am a verb-*noun*.'
a gerund grieves for its lost identity

In examples such as those, the adjectival function of the present participle is so dominant that it may be described simply as an adjective.

You will not confuse the present participle with the gerund if you remember that a word *is* what it *does* in a sentence.

Examples

1 *Asking* three thousand pounds is excessive. (gerund)
2 Their *asking* price of three thousand pounds is excessive. (present participle)

In Sentence 1, the verb-form *Asking* is the subject-word of the verb 'is'. It therefore functions as a noun and it is a gerund. In Sentence 2, the verb-form *asking* qualifies the noun 'price'. It therefore functions as an adjective and it is a present participle.

(d) The past participle

Like the present participle, the past participle functions as a *verb-adjective*, but it does not end in *-ing*. The past participle often ends in *-ed*, *-en*, *-d* or *-t*.

Examples

Verb	Part participle
to talk	talk*ed*
to beat	beat*en*
to sell	sol*d*
to sleep	slep*t*

The past participle may be formed by a vowel change.

Examples

Verb	Past participle
to ring	rung
to bind	bound

Or there may be no change.

Examples

Verb	Past participle
to set	set
to hit	hit
to put	put

When its function is to qualify a noun or a pronoun, the past participle may be described simply as an adjective.

Examples

1 That winter, the milk was *frozen.*
2 The *tarred* road melted in the sun.
3 A *bound* volume of essays was presented to the lecturer.

7.3 PARTICIPIAL PHRASES

Participial phrases play an important and prominent part in the grammar of the simple sentence.

Examples

1 *Living in the country*, I have a long journey to work. The present participle 'Living' introduces a participial phrase. The participial phrase *Living in the country* qualifies the pronoun 'I'. It functions as an adjective-phrase.

2 We spoke to the man *standing at the back*.

The present participle 'standing' introduces a participial phrase. The participial phrase *standing at the back* qualifies the noun 'man'. It functions as an adjective-phrase.

3 The plants, *beaten down by the heavy rain*, were a sorry sight.

The past participle 'beaten' introduces a participial phrase. The participial phrase *beaten down by the heavy rain* qualifies the noun 'plants'. It functions as an adjective-phrase.

4 *Bored by the long speech*, the audience slept.

The past participle 'Bored' introduces a participial phrase. The participial phrase *Bored by the long speech* qualifies the noun 'audience'. It functions as an adjective-phrase.

REMEMBER

- A participial phrase is a group of words forming part of a simple sentence. It is introduced by a participle (either a present participle or a past participle). It qualifies a noun or a pronoun elsewhere in the sentence. Thus, a participial phrase functions as an adjective.

In addition to the functions discussed here, the present participle and the past participle are used to denote tense and 'voice'.

Examples

1 I am writing. (present continuous tense: active voice)
2 I have written. (present perfect tense: active voice)
3 The letter was written. (past simple tense: passive voice)

These matters will be dealt with in Chapter 12 and need not be gone into here, where we are concerned only with the function of participles in sentences.

Test 34
Answers on page 168.
Describe the function of the infinitive verb-form in each of these sentences.

Example

We have some spare vegetables to sell.

The infinitive *to sell* qualifies the noun 'vegetables'. It functions as an adjective.

1 To climb safely requires experience.
2 They are ready to start.
3 The explorers wanted to return by air.
4 Have you anything to declare?
5 To work is to pray.

Test 35

Answers on page 168.

Classify the italicised words as either gerunds or present participles. Give reasons.

1 *Taking* corners too fast is a frequent cause of accidents.
2 He was led away *shouting.*
3 The *thieving* children are a menace at that station.
4 The gang was notorious for its *thieving*.
5 The crops are ripe for *harvesting*.

Test 36

Answers on page 168.

Identify each participial phrase and describe its function.

1 Alarmed by the trade figures, the government increased taxes.
2 Sleeping so near the road, I had many a restless night.
3 Who was the announcer reading the six o'clock news?
4 Tired of waiting, the crowd grew restless.
5 That cake was in a parcel posted by my mother.

Like the present and past participles, the other two non-finite forms of the verb – the gerund and the infinitive – may introduce phrases.

A full description of gerundive and infinitive phrases is provided in Section 8.4, where all the different kinds of phrases are explained and analysed. However, a brief account of gerundive and infinitive phrases is useful here to distinguish them from participial phrases.

7.4 GERUNDIVE PHRASES

A gerundive phrase is introduced by a gerund and it functions as a noun in the sentence to which it belongs. It can be the subject or the direct object or the complement of a verb.

Examples

1 PRACTISING for seven hours a day perfected his skill.

The gerundive phrase PRACTISING for seven hours a day is the subject of the verb 'perfected'.

2 He bitterly regretted MAKING an enemy of her.

The gerundive phrase MAKING an enemy of her is the direct object of the verb 'regretted'.

3 Her hobby is COLLECTING old photographs.

The gerundive phrase COLLECTING old photographs is used predicatively. It functions as a noun-phrase and completes the predicate of the verb 'is'.

As we saw in Section 7.2(b), a gerund can follow a preposition, thus forming part of a prepositional phrase.

Example

The child upset its grandparents by TALKING loudly.

It can be argued that TALKING loudly is a gerundive phrase following the preposition 'by'; but that is not a very illuminating description. We learn much more about the structure of that sentence if we consider by TALKING loudly as a complete phrase, all the words in which work *together*. We then see quite clearly that by TALKING loudly is a prepositional phrase modifying the verb 'upset' and, therefore, functioning as an adverb. That accurate description in no way obscures the verb-noun nature of the gerund TALKING, which functions as the noun in the prepositional phrase *and* retains the nature of a verb by denoting action and by being itself modified by the adverb 'loudly'.

7.5 INFINITIVE PHRASES

An infinitive phrase is introduced by an infinitive. In its sentence it can function as: a noun *or* an adjective *or* an adverb.

Examples

1 TO WIN the pools is an unlikely solution of a financial crisis.

The infinitive phrase TO WIN the pools is the subject of the verb 'is'. It functions as a noun.

2 The chancellor decided TO RISK an inflationary budget.

The infinitive phrase TO RISK an inflationary budget is the direct object of the verb 'decided'. It functions as a noun.

3 In later years, he was TO LOSE his inspired touch.

The infinitive phrase TO LOSE his inspired touch is the complement of the verb 'was'. It functions as a predicative noun.

4 There is no money TO SPARE for luxuries.

The infinitive phrase TO SPARE for luxuries qualifies the noun 'money'. It functions as an adjective.

5 We got ready TO GO to bed.

The infinitive phrase TO GO to bed modifies the adjective 'ready', which is a predicative adjective completing the predicate of the verb 'got'. The infinitive phrase functions as an adverb.

CHAPTER 8

SIMPLE SENTENCE ANALYSIS

The purpose of analysis is to make the complete grammatical structure of a sentence clear. Each part of the sentence is identified, its function described, and its relationship to the other parts of the sentence explained.

There are different ways of presenting a sentence analysis. The way you do it is up to you, but your chosen scheme must be comprehensive and clear.

8.1 TABULAR ANALYSIS

The table set out in Section 6.9 will do very well, though economy of space can be achieved by using one column for the object. A direct object is identified thus: (D). An indirect object is identified thus: (I).

A distinction must also be made (in the predicative words column) between a 'subjective complement' and an 'objective complement'. The former, labelled (SC), follows a being verb and refers to the subject. The latter, labelled (OC), follows the direct object of an action verb and refers to that object (Section 6.8).

Examples of tabular analysis

1 The scientific society awarded the learned scholar its gold medal at its annual general meeting.
2 This is the most entertaining play of the year.
3 After a lot of trouble, we got the pump working efficiently.

Subject		Predicate				
subject-word	*adjectives or adjective-phrases qualifying subject-word*	*verb*	*adverbs or adverb phrases modifying verb*	*object-word*	*adjectives or adjective-phrases qualifying object-word*	*predicative word + words qualifying/ modifying predicative word*
1 society	the scientific	awarded	at its annual general meeting	medal (D) scholar (I)	its gold the learned	
2 this		is				play (SC) + the most entertaining of the year
3 we		got	after a lot of trouble	pump (D)	the	working (OC) + efficiently

8.2 DESCRIPTIVE ANALYSIS

We have used descriptive analysis on many occasions in this book. It is a useful explanatory method of bringing out the facts of sentence structure.

Examples of descriptive analysis

1 The farmer's plans required a great deal of capital in the first few years.

SUBJECT
subject-word: plans
adjectives or adjective-phrases qualifying subject-word: the farmer's
PREDICATE
verb: required
adverbs or adverb-phrases modifying verb: in the first few years
direct object-word: deal
adjectives or adjective-phrases qualifying direct object-word: a great; of capital

2 Can you spare me ten minutes of your valuable time?

SUBJECT
subject-word: you
PREDICATE
verb: can spare
direct object-word: minutes
adjectives or adjective-phrases qualifying direct object-word: ten; of your valuable time
indirect object-word: me

3 In due course, they handed the anxious traveller his passport.

SUBJECT

subject-word: they

PREDICATE

verb: handed

adverbs or adverb-phrases modifying verb: in due course

direct object-word: passport

adjectives or adjective-phrases qualifying direct-object word: his

indirect object-word: traveller

adjectives or adjective-phrases qualifying indirect object-word: the anxious

4 I visited that little church, a beautiful building, last year.

SUBJECT

subject-word: I

PREDICATE

verb: visited

adverbs or adverb-phrases modifying verb: last year

direct object-word: church/building

adjectives or adjective-phrases qualifying direct object-word: that little/a beautiful

Sentence 4 illustrates a grammatical feature called *apposition*. When two nouns name the same person, thing or idea, they are described as being 'in apposition' to each other.

Examples

1 The intended *victim*, a professional *wrestler*, soon overpowered his assailants.

The two nouns in the subject, *victim* and *wrestler*, name the same person, so they are in apposition to each other.

2 The job went to the most experienced *candidate*, a middle-aged *woman*.

The two nouns in the predicate, *candidate* and *woman*, name the same person, so they are in apposition to each other.

Note the punctuation of the appositional words. In Example 1, two commas mark off the second noun from the first. In Example 2, one comma performs the same function.

Opinions differ as to how nouns in apposition should be presented in analysis. The descriptive analysis of Sentence 4, just given, illustrates one view: that since the two nouns name the same person, thing or idea, they should be placed in the same category. The analysis was, therefore, *direct object-word*: church/building.

The other view is that the second of the two nouns functions as an adjective qualifying the first. According to that view, the analysis should be:

direct object-word: church
adjectives and adjective-phrases qualifying direct object-word: that little/a beautiful building

The second view has much to recommend it, for nouns often function as adjectives.

Examples

1 We bought the *evening* paper.
2 The *London* train leaves at five.
3 *Fred's* coat was torn on the wire.
4 The *government's* policies are discredited.

Whichever of those two classifications you adopt for the second of two nouns in apposition, you will not be considered wrong, provided that your analysis sets out your classification clearly and explains the reasoning behind it.

The two methods of presenting analysis so far discussed have their respective strong and weak points.

Tabular analysis (Section 8.1) sets out at its head all the parts that may be present in a simple sentence. This comprehensive list provides a useful checking procedure. As we are analysing, we can see at a glance the columns in which entries have been made. An empty column alerts us to the possibility that we have omitted an item or misplaced one.

On the other hand, the tabular method, when used for simple sentences, makes analysis seem to be a mechanical, cut-and-dried process. Such a view is unfortunately common, but completely erroneous. Analysis is – or should be – a sensitive grammatical exploration of the structure of a sentence.

Descriptive analysis (Section 8.2) involves us very actively with the sentences that we are exploring. It encourages us to reason out the function of each successive part of the sentence while seeing it in its full grammatical context. It is, however, more time-consuming than tabular analysis, and many students of grammar find it laborious.

The method known as 'graphic analysis' has many advantages, not the least of these being the fact that it presents grammatical relationships in a lively fashion. Once its simple conventional signs have been learnt, it is easy to apply to any simple sentence and – properly used – it is clear, accurate and vivid.

8.3 GRAPHIC ANALYSIS

The conventional signs of graphic analysis are set out in sections (a) to (h) below. Each sign identifies a grammatical relationship and function with which you are now familiar. As you will see, a system of signs is available to provide a full account of the grammar of the simple sentence.

(a) Subject-word + verb
Sentence for analysis: We laughed.
Graphic analysis

Subject	Predicate
we ——	—— laughed

(b) Subject-word + qualifiers of subject-word
Sentence for analysis: The old man snored.
Graphic analysis

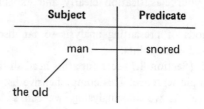

(c) Verb + modifiers of verb
Sentence for analysis: Swallows fly fast.
Graphic analysis

Subject	Predicate
swallows ——	—— fly
	fast

(d) Verb + direct object-word
Sentence for analysis: They have invited me.
Graphic analysis

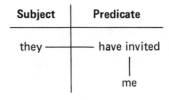

(e) Verb + indirect object-word
Sentence for analysis: She gave me tea.
Graphic analysis

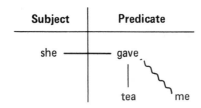

(f) Verb + predicative word(s)
Sentence for analysis: She is very determined.
Graphic analysis

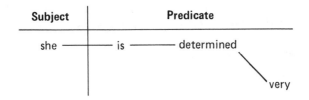

(g) The basic diagram of graphic analysis
As you have seen in (a) to (f), the conventional signs of graphic analysis provide a diagrammatic method of presenting each stage of a simple sentence analysis. Here is the basic diagram on which the method depends.

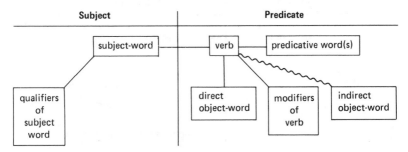

(h) The flexibility of graphic analysis

The convenience of the graphic method is increased by its flexibility. Using only the basic conventional signs, we can apply the method to any simple sentence to highlight any particular grammatical features that we want to explore in detail.

Examples

1 These new regulations are completely absurd.
Graphic analysis

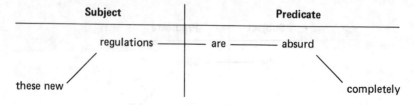

The predicative word 'absurd' is an adjective completing the predicate of the verb 'are' and referring to the subject-word 'regulations'. The word 'completely' tells us more about the predicative adjective 'absurd'. Therefore, it is an adverb modifying 'absurd'.

That accurate, but wordy, description of the grammatical functions of those words and of the relationships between them is represented swiftly and clearly by the conventional signs of graphic analysis.

2 The documents arrived in an envelope secured by red sealing-wax.
Graphic analysis

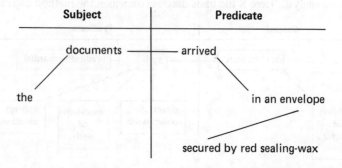

The prepositional phrase 'in an envelope' is an adverb-phrase modifying the verb 'arrived'. The participial phrase 'secured by red sealing-wax' tells us more about the noun 'envelope'. Therefore, it is an adjective-phrase qualifying 'envelope'.

3 We sent poor old Jimmy a cheque at Christmas.
Graphic analysis

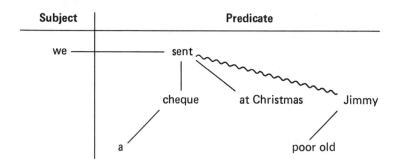

4 We sent poor old Jimmy a cheque for Christmas.
Graphic analysis

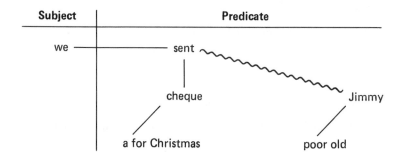

in Example 3, the prepositional phrase 'at Christmas' is an adverb-phrase modifying the verb 'sent'. In Example 4, the prepositional phrase 'for Christmas' is an adjective-phrase qualifying the noun 'cheque'.

As those four examples show, the graphic method is economical and vivid. One of its particular advantages is the use of the adjective-sign / and the adverb-sign \ to display qualifying and modifying items, either in the subject or in the predicate.

Direct object vertical line; indirect obj. squiggle at 30°.

Test 37

Answers on page 168.

Make a graphic analysis of each of these sentences.

1 Ten thousand visitors from all over the world will see these rare pictures this year.

2 Jane's captaincy of the first team seemed pretty good to me on Saturday.

3 Nothing can bring them help now.

4 Within ten minutes, the orator on the platform became inaudible at the back of the hall.

5 Lovers of a good film gave that moving picture a rapturous reception.

8.4 ANALYSING PHRASES

Badly constructed and misplaced phrases are often the cause of grammatical blunders (see Chapter 13). Practice in phrase analysis helps us to avoid such blunders by teaching us to recognise the structures and functions of phrases of different kinds.

- As we have seen, a phrase is a group of words (two or more) that does *not* make complete sense *on its own* because it does *not* contain a *finite* verb.
- As part of a sentence, a phrase functions as a noun, *or* as an adjective *or* as an adverb.

Examples

1 *To exceed the speed limit* is dangerous.

The phrase is the subject of the verb 'is'. Therefore, it functions as a noun-phrase.

2 She would like a camera *of her own*.

The phrase qualifies the noun 'camera'. Therefore, it functions as an adjective-phrase.

3 We found the money *just in time*.

The phrase modifies the verb 'found'. Therefore, it functions as an adverb-phrase.

We classified the phrases in those examples *functionally*, according to the word that they did in their sentences.

Phrases may also be classified *structurally*, according to their introductory words. By identifying the word or words at the beginning of the phrase, we can recognise the structure of the phrase. We can then go on to describe the function of the phrase in the sentence.

(a) A prepositional phrase begins with a preposition

Examples

1 That problem is BEYOND my skill.

The prepositional phrase BEYOND my skill completes the predicate of the verb 'is' and refers to the subject-word 'problem'. Therefore, it functions as a predicative adjective-phrase.

2 The flood water raced THROUGH the street.

The prepositional phrase THROUGH the street modifies the verb 'raced'. Therefore, it functions as an adverb-phrase.

(b) A participial phrase begins with a participal (present or past)

Examples

1 ARRIVING late, the travellers missed their evening meal.

The (present) participial phrase ARRIVING late qualifies the noun 'travellers'. Therefore, it functions as an adjective-phrase.

2 The successful candidates commiserated with those ELIMINATED earlier.

The (past) participial phrase ELIMINATED earlier qualifies the pronoun 'those'. Therefore, it functions as an adjective-phrase.

(c) An infinitive phrase begins with an infinitive

Examples

1 TO KEEP their attention would be a considerable feat.

The infinitive phrase TO KEEP their attention is the subject of the verb 'would be'. Therefore, it functions as a noun-phrase.

2 He tried TO HIDE the evidence.

The infinitive phrase TO HIDE the evidence is the direct object of the verb 'tried'. Therefore, it functions as a noun-phrase.

3 That is a device TO REDUCE petrol consumption.

The infinitive phrase TO REDUCE petrol consumption qualifies the noun 'device'. Therefore, it functions as an adjective-phrase: a fact quickly established by graphic analysis.

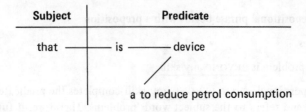

Subject	Predicate
that —— is —— device	
	a to reduce petrol consumption

4 We climbed the tower TO SEE the view.

The infinitive phrase TO SEE the view modifies the verb 'climbed'. (It tells us the purpose for which the action was performed.) Therefore, it functions as an adverb-phrase.

5 Four of the present team seem certain TO PLAY next week.

The infinitive phrase TO PLAY next week modifies the adjective 'certain'. Therefore, it functions as an adverb-phrase.

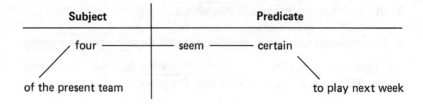

Subject	Predicate
four —— seem —— certain	
of the present team	to play next week

Note The subject-word 'four' is a pronoun (of *number* or *quantity* – see Chapter 12). The prepositional phrase 'of the present team' is an adjective-phrase qualifying that pronoun.

(d) A gerundive phrase begins with a gerund

Examples

1 WORKING hard was his recipe for long life.

The gerundive phrase WORKING hard is the subject of the verb 'was'. Therefore, it functions as a noun-phrase.

2 She enjoys PLAYING the piano.

The gerundive phrase PLAYING the piano is the direct object of the verb 'enjoys'. Therefore, it functions as a noun-phrase.

3 Their speciality was DESIGNING fast boats.

The gerundive phrase DESIGNING fast boats completes the predicate of the verb 'was' and refers to the subject-word 'speciality'. Therefore, it functions as a predicative noun-phrase.

Note Graphic analysis is a most useful way of bringing out the distinction between gerundive phrases and (present) participial phrases.

Examples

1 Working hard was his recipe for long life.
Graphic analysis

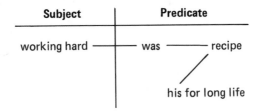

2 Working hard, he lived a long life.
Graphic analysis

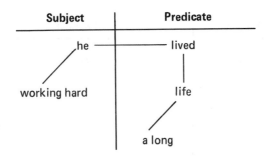

(e) An adverbial phrase begins with an adverb
It is important to remember that other kinds of phrases can do the work of an adverb. The structural classification 'adverbial phrase' applies only to phrases that begin with an adverb and have an adverb-phrase function.

Examples

1 You have kept these books MUCH too long.

The adverbial phrase MUCH too long modifies the verb 'have kept'. Therefore, it functions as an adverb-phrase.

A graphic analysis brings out the adverbial function of *all* the words in the phrase.

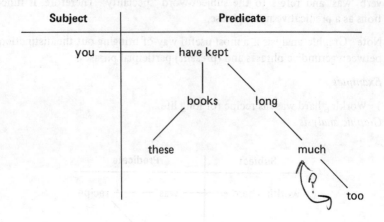

Compare this sentence with the next example:

2 The blow was very painful indeed.

A graphic analysis shows that 'very painful indeed' is *not* an adverbial phrase.

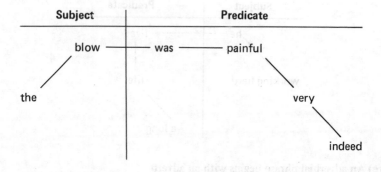

The word 'painful' completes the predicate of the verb 'was' and it refers to the subject-word 'blow'. Therefore, 'painful' is a predicative adjective. The two words 'very' and 'indeed' modify the predicative adjective. Therefore, they function as adverbs.

Compare again:

3 They completed the course VERY easily indeed.

In this sentence VERY easily indeed is an adverbial phrase modifying the verb 'completed'. It is an adverbial phrase because: (i) it begins with an adverb (very) and (ii) *every* word in the phrase functions as an adverb. (Contrast 'very painful indeed' in Example 2.)

REMEMBER

- An adverbial phrase begins with an adverb.
- All the words in the phrase function as adverbs.
- Adverbial phrases occur only in the predicate.

A thorough understanding of the grammar of phrases is an essential preliminary to the study of *clauses*, which are introduced in Chapter 9.

CLAUSES AND SENTENCES

9.1 WHAT IS A CLAUSE?

So far, we have been studying the grammar of the simple sentence: that is, a sentence containing one (and only one) finite verb. In other words, a sentence containing one subject and one predicate.

Many sentences, however, contain more than one finite verb. Such sentences consist of two or more groups of words, each of which has a subject and predicate of its own.

Examples

1a   The weather *was* fine.
1b   We *walked* every day.
1c   The weather *was* fine and we *walked* every day.

The two simple sentences, 1a and 1b, are linked by the conjunction 'and' to form sentence 1c, which contains two finite verbs ('was' and 'walked').

Therefore, sentence 1c contains two subjects and two predicates. Its structure is:

Subject 1 and Predicate 1 + Link + Subject 2 and Predicate 2

the weather   was fine   +   and +   we   walked every day

Each simple sentence has become *part of* another sentence. In so doing, it ceased to be a sentence and became a *clause*.

REMEMBER

- A *clause* is a group of words containing a subject and predicate *of its own* and forming *part of* a sentence.

In the terms of that definition, the structure of sentence 1c is:

Clause 1   + **Link**   + **Clause 2**

the weather was fine + and   + we walked every day

9.2 MAIN CLAUSES

Each of the two clauses in sentence 1c can stand on its own and make sense without the help of the other clause. A clause of that kind is called a *main* clause.

REMEMBER

- A clause that makes sense without the help of another clause is a *main* clause.

Examples of main clauses

1 They searched the spy's room / but / they did not find his radio.
2 The electrician pressed the switch / and / the motor started.
3 Shall I take the train / or / (shall I take) the bus?

In all three sentences, either of the two clauses makes sense on its own and all three sentences are constructed on the same pattern:

       main clause 1   +   link   +   main clause 2

9.3 CO-ORDINATING CONJUNCTIONS

In the sentences just examined, each of the conjunctions 'but', 'and' and 'or' links two main clauses. Conjunctions doing that work are called *co-ordinating* conjunctions because they link *co-ordinate* clauses. 'Co-ordinate' clauses are clauses that are of equal 'standing' or 'rank'. They are equal in rank because they do similar jobs in the sentence of which they form a part.

REMEMBER

- A *co-ordinating* conjunction links two clauses of *equal* rank. In other words, it links *co-ordinate* clauses.

9.4 DOUBLE SENTENCES

We have already had several examples of double sentences:

1 The weather was fine and we walked every day.
2 They searched the spy's room but they did not find his radio.

3 The electrician pressed the switch and the motor started.
4 Shall I take the train or (shall I take) the bus?

Each of those sentences has the same structure:

main clause 1 + co-ordinating conjunction + main clause 2

It is easy to see that a double sentence is basically two simple sentences linked together by a co-ordinating conjunction. Of course, when they are linked together to form one sentence, the simple sentences are no longer sentences: they become clauses when they become parts of a sentence.

Two further facts about double sentences must be noted:

1 When the subject of the second clause is the same as the subject of the first clause, it is often omitted. It becomes an 'understood' subject.
2 Like a simple sentence, a double sentence may contain phrases.

Example

Trusting the weather forecast, we left our raincoats in the hotel and returned at four o'clock, drenched to the skin.

main clause 1:   'Trusting. . .hotel'
link: 'and'
main clause 2:   '(we) returned. . .skin'
phrase 1:   'trusting the weather forecast' (adjective-phrase qualifying pronoun 'we', subject of verb 'left' in main clause 1)
phrase 2:   'in the hotel' (adverb-phrase modifying verb 'left' in main clause 1)
phrase 3:   'at four o'clock' (adverb-phrase modifying verb 'returned' in main clause 2)
phrase 4:   'drenched to the skin' (adjective-phrase qualifying [understood] pronoun 'we', subject of verb 'returned' in main clause 2)

Sometimes, the second verb is omitted as well as the second subject, as in one of our earlier examples:

Shall I take the train or the bus?

It is clear that the two clauses in that sentence are:
main clause 1:   Shall I take the train?
link: or
main clause 2:   (shall) (I) (take) the bus?

Test 38
Answers on page 169.
Identify these sentences as simple or double. (If there is one finite verb, the sentence is simple.)

1 The path through the woods was closed some years ago, but I know of a way in.

2 At the foot of Sticklepath Hill, behind a clump of bushes, you will see a stile.

3 The stile leads to an overgrown track and you must be careful to keep to it.

4 Neither the turning to the right, by the tumbledown hut, nor the left fork at Robbers' Beech, will lead you through the woods.

5 The route is, in fact, rather difficult to find, but following it will reward you with the best woodland scenery in this district.

9.5 MULTIPLE SENTENCES

A multiple sentence is constructed in the same way as a double sentence. The only difference is that a multiple sentence contains *more than two* main clauses.

Example

I have spent half an hour on grammar and I have written an essay, but I still have some work to do.

Three main clauses:	1 'I...grammar'
	2 'I...essay'
	3 'I...do'
Two co-ordinating conjunctions:	1 'and'
	2 'but'

As in double sentences, repetition is often avoided by omitting a subject-word when it is clear that the subject of all the clauses is the same.

Example

She sat down and (she) started to read, but (she) went to sleep.

Often, a co-ordinating conjunction is omitted and replaced by a comma.

Example

She sat down, started to read, but went to sleep.

Such omissions have no effect on the grammar of a multiple sentence. The example just given consists of three main clauses linked by two co-ordinating conjunctions.

main clause 1:   'She sat down'
co-ordinating conjunction 1 (understood):   '(and)'
main clause 2:   '(she) started to read'

co-ordinating conjunction 2:   'but'
main clause 3:   '(she) went to sleep'

Test 39
Answers on page 170.
Say whether these sentences are simple, double or multiple.

1 He sat quietly in a corner of the room and listened to the animated conversation.

2 Robin Hood drew his bow, loosed the shaft and brought down the deer.

3 Desperate for money, the company chairman, with blatant disregard of the rules drawn up a year before, authorised the sale of products awaiting the clearance of quality control.

9.6 COMPLEX SENTENCES

So far, we have discussed only main clauses. The study of complex sentences introduces us to clauses of a different kind.

Examples of complex sentences:

1 She felt sorry for her aunt when she read her letter.
2 They rewarded the man who rescued their son.
3 A quick-witted dealer bought the car that I wanted.

There are two clauses in each of those sentences:

Sentence 1
clause (a):   She felt sorry for her aunt
clause (b):   when she read her letter
Sentence 2
clause (a):   They rewarded the man
clause (b):   who rescued their son
Sentence 3
clause (a):   A quick-witted dealer bought the car
clause (b) :   that I wanted

In each sentence, the (a) clause makes complete sense without the help of the other clause. It could stand alone.

In each sentence, the (b) clause does not make complete sense without the help of the other clause. It could not stand alone.

The clause that could make sense on its own is called the *main* clause. The clause that needs the help of the main clause is called the *subordinate* clause.

REMEMBER

- A sentence that contains one main clause and at least one subordinate clause is a complex sentence.

Since 'main clause' and 'subordinate clause' are not the only terms in use, the following points must be borne in mind.

1 A *main* clause makes the main statement in a sentence, hence the term 'main'. It is sometimes called an *independent* clause because it does not depend on any other clause for help in making a complete statement.
2 A *subordinate* clause is 'lower in rank' than a main clause, hence the term 'subordinate'. It is sometimes called a *dependent* clause because it depends on the main clause to help it to express its meaning in the sentence. It cannot make a complete statement on its own.
3 It is convenient to standardise terms wherever possible. Since most writers on grammar use the terms *main clause* and *subordinate clause*, those are the terms that will be used in this book.
4 There is nothing 'wrong' with the alternative terms, *independent clause* and *dependent* clause. Indeed, as we have just seen, they are accurate descriptions of the different functions of the two kinds of clauses.

Test 40
Answers on page 170.
Classify each of these sentences as simple, double, multiple or complex.

1 Mr Brown placed the guard in front of the kitchen fire, put the cat out, switched off all the downstairs lights and went to bed.
2 Hoping not to be disturbed, I sat down in my easy chair and started to read.
3 Hoping not to be disturbed, I sat down in my easy chair and started to read the book that I won as a prize.
4 Considering how to win badly-needed votes, the government introduced tax reliefs just before the election.
5 Jack, whose attention always wandered after the first few minutes, was startled by the sudden question.

9.7 KINDS OF SENTENCES: A CHECK-LIST

When you looked up the answers to Test 40, you may have found that you had misclassified some of the sentences. Here is a check list of steps to follow when you are classifying sentences. As you study it you will realise that it is the number of *main* clauses that determines the sentence type.

	Ask these questions	Draw these conclusions
1	How many finite verbs are there in this sentence?	There are as many clauses as there are finite verbs: one clause for every finite verb.
2	Is there only one finite verb in this sentence?	If so, the sentence is a simple sentence.
3	Are there two or more finite verbs in this sentence?	If so, the sentence is not a simple sentence.
4	Is there one main clause and at least one subordinate clause in this sentence?	If so, the sentence is a complex sentence.
5	Are there two main clauses and no subordinate clauses in this sentence?	If so, the sentence is a double sentence.
6	Are there two main clauses and at least one subordinate clause in this sentence?	If so, the sentence is a double sentence.
7	Are there more than two main clauses and no subordinate clauses in this sentence?	If so, the sentence is a multiple sentence.
8	Are there more than two main clauses and at least one subordinate clause in this sentence?	If so, the sentence is a multiple sentence.

9.8 SUMMING UP

Kind of sentence	Distinguishing features
Simple sentence	*one* finite verb
Complex sentence	*one* main clause AND *one or more* subordinate clauses
Double sentence	*two* main clauses WITH OR WITHOUT one or more subordinate clauses
Multiple sentence	*more than two* main clauses WITH OR WITHOUT one or more subordinate clauses

SUBORDINATE CLAUSES AND THE WORK THEY DO

10.1 INTRODUCTION

As we now know, phrases function as adjectives, as adverbs or as nouns in the sentences to which they belong. An adjective-phrase is an adjective equivalent, an adverb-phrase is an adverb equivalent and a noun-phrase is a noun equivalent.

Subordinate clauses function in the same ways as phrases. They, too, are adjective, adverb or noun equivalents.

The fundamental difference between a phrase and a subordinate clause is that a phrase does not contain a finite verb, whereas a subordinate clause does. That is to say, a subordinate clause has a subject and a predicate of its own.

The possession of a subject and a predicate of its own does not confer independence on a subordinate clause. A subordinate clause always refers to a word (or a group of words) in *another* clause. That other clause may be either a main clause or another subordinate clause.

In either case, the function of the subordinate clause is determined by its relationship to the word (or group of words) to which it refers in that other clause.

To discover the function of a subordinate clause we have to identify the word (or group of words) with which the subordinate clause is linked; and we have to discover the nature of the link.

We have to ask (and answer) this question:

- What exactly is the relationship between this subordinate clause and that word (or group of words) in the other clause?

In order to simplify our demonstration of the work that each kind of subordinate clause does, our examples in this chapter are based on complex sentences containing one subordinate clause. In Chapter 11 we shall analyse complex sentences containing more than one subordinate clause.

There, too, we shall analyse double and multiple sentences each containing more than one subordinate clause.

We begin with adjective-clauses because they present few difficulties, while providing a clear demonstration of the basic function common to all subordinate clauses.

We then go on to adverb-clauses. They are not difficult to identify, for they always function as adverbs. There are, however, several different kinds of adverb-clauses which require explanation.

Finally, we come to noun-clauses, which have special features. Our work on the two other kinds of subordinate clauses serves as a helpful introduction to these.

10.2 ADJECTIVE-CLAUSES

(a) Qualifying the subject-word in another clause
Consider these three sentences:

1 Illustrated books sell well at Christmas.
2 Books with illustrations sell well at Christmas.
3 Books that have illustrations sell well at Christmas.

Sentence 3 is a complex sentence. It has one main clause: 'Books sell well at Christmas'. It has one subordinate clause: 'that have illustrations'.

With which word in the main clause is the subordinate clause linked? What exactly is the relationship between the subordinate clause and the word in the main clause with which it is linked?

The answers to those two questions are not hard to find. The subordinate clause 'that have illustrations' is linked to the word 'books' in the main clause. The subordinate clause qualifies (describes, tells us more about) 'books'. In its own clause, 'books' is a noun. It is the subject-word of the verb 'sell'.

In fact, the subordinate clause does exactly the same work as the adjective 'illustrated' in Sentence 1 and exactly the same work as the adjective-phrase 'with illustrations' in Sentence 2.

Our conclusion must be that the subordinate clause is an adjective-clause qualifying the noun 'books', which is the subject-word in the other clause.

We can make use of tabular analysis to express those facts:

Clause	Kind	Function
books sell well at Christmas	main	
that have illustrations	subordinate adjective-clause	qualifies noun *books* in main clause

We shall return to tabular analysis in Chapter 11 and see how it can be built up into a complete system capable of describing more complicated sentences than those we shall analyse in this chapter. It is worth noticing here that the 'function column' is left blank for a main clause. A main clause *always* makes the main statement, so its function need not be entered in the table.

Test 41
Answers on page 170.
Identify the adjective-clauses in these sentences. State the word that each qualifies.

1 Politicians who toe the party line generally get on.
2 Cars that have diesel engines are becoming popular.
3 The route that you recommended was not easy to follow.
4 His excuses, which were not convincing, angered his sister.
5 Telephone directories from which pages are missing must be replaced.
Note The punctuation in Sentence 4 illustrates a grammatical point that will be dealt with in Chapter 13.

(b) Qualifying the direct object-word in another clause
Since the direct object-word must be a noun *or* a pronoun *or* a noun equivalent, a subordinate clause that qualifies a direct object-word must be an adjective-clause.

Examples

1 The organisers invited entries that did not exceed 1000 words.
2 Did you see the man who was asking for you?
3 I made the dress that I intend to wear.

Here is a tabular analysis of the first of those examples.

Clause	Kind	Function
the organisers invited entries	main	
that did not exceed 1000 words	subordinate adjective-clause	qualifies noun *entries* in main clause

In the second example, the adjective-clause 'who was asking for you' qualifies the noun 'man', which is the direct object-word in the main clause. In the third example, the adjective-clause 'that I intend to wear' qualifies the noun 'dress', which is the direct object-word in the main clause.

(c) Qualifying the indirect object-word in another clause

The noun, pronoun or noun equivalent functioning as the indirect object-word may be qualified by an adjective-clause.

Examples

1 I sent my sister, who was going to live in the country, some of my favourite records.
2 The craftsman offered the apprentice who arrived last week lessons in carving.
3 We promised the committee, which was newly elected, our full support.
Note The punctuation of these sentences will be discussed in Chapter 13.

In example 1, the subordinate clause 'who was going to live in the country' is an adjective-clause qualifying the noun 'sister' (which is the indirect object-word in the main clause).

Similarly, in example 2, the subordinate clause is an adjective-clause qualifying the noun 'apprentice'.

In example 3, the subordinate clause is an adjective-clause qualifying the noun 'committee'.

(d) Qualifying a noun, pronoun or noun equivalent in the complement of another clause

Examples

1 For over twenty years, she was the STAR *who filled this theatre.*
2 That day was ONE *that I shall never forget.*
3 Eventually, he became a trusted ADVISER *upon whom this firm depended.*
Note In example 3, the adjective-clause is introduced by the preposition 'upon'.

(e) Adjective-clauses and their introducers/links

As our examples have shown, adjective-clauses are introduced by a word that also serves to link them to a word in the other clause: 'She is a singer *whom* we all admire'.

Adjective-clauses frequently begin with one of the following words: who, whom, whose, which, that, as, where, when, why. It is never safe, however, to try to identify a clause simply by the word with which it begins. Some of the words in the list just given can introduce clauses of different kinds. A clause can be identified only by its function in the sentence of which it is a part.

REMEMBER

- A clause *is* what it DOES in a sentence.

The introducing/linking word that leads into an adjective-clause is a relative pronoun *or* a relative adjective *or* a relative adverb (see Chapter 12).

The introducing/linking word may itself be preceded by a preposition. We have already had one example of that. Here are two more: 'These are the rules BY *which we live*', 'That was the year IN *which he discovered his talents.*'

It is important to remember that the introducing/linking word may be omitted. This is quite common in English.

Examples

1 She is an author you will not have read.

Main clause: She is an author
Adjective-clause: (whom) you will not have read

2 I must post the letter I have just written.

Main clause: I must post the letter
Adjective-clause: (that) I have just written

As you see from those examples, the omission of the introducing/linking word in no way affects the grammar of the sentence.

Often, the introducing/linking word cannot be omitted from the beginning of the adjective-clause without destroying the sense of the sentence.

Examples

1 Our host showed us his garden *which* grew some remarkable shrubs.
2 The minister *who* prepared the legislation was forced to resign.

(f) Adjective-clauses and their antecedents

The noun, pronoun or noun equivalent in another clause to which a subordinate adjective-clause refers and which it qualifies is called the *antecedent* of the adjective-clause.

It is the function of the introducing/linking word with which the adjective-clause begins to *relate* to the antecedent and to link the adjective-clause to it.

That is why the introducing/linking words are called *relative* pronouns, adjectives or adverbs (see Chapter 12).

Examples

(The antecedents are printed in italics.)
1 I showed my passport to the *officer* who was standing at the barrier.
2 They took *decisions* which they never explained.
3 A *house* that is too large is a burden.

A misplaced or ambiguous antecedent is a frequent source of error in speech and in writing (see Chapter 13).

(g) Summing up

REMEMBER

- Adjective-clauses have their own subject and predicate, but their function is to qualify a noun, pronoun or noun equivalent in *another* clause.
- That clause may be either a main clause or a subordinate clause.

Examples

1 We never discovered the method *they used to cheat the firm*.

The adjective-clause qualifies the noun 'method' in the main clause.

2 This model, *which is bought by farmers who have large areas to spray*, is not suitable for private gardens.

There are two subordinate adjective-clauses here. The first, 'which is bought by farmers', qualifies the noun 'model' in the main clause. The second, 'who have large areas to spray', qualifies the noun 'farmers' in the first subordinate clause.

Test 42

Answers on page 170.
Identify the adjective-clauses. State the antecedent of the introducing/linking word with which each clause begins.

1 The book that I had placed on the table was no longer there.
2 The boy who found the wallet was rewarded.

3 She is an author whom I have enjoyed.
4 Who will continue the work which he has begun?
5 That is a play I saw in London last year.

10.3 ADVERB-CLAUSES

(a) Introduction

There are ten different kinds of adverb-clauses, and the attempt to learn those categories by heart has proved too much for many a student of English grammar.

The attempt is misguided. It is a perfect example of putting the cart before the horse. What matters first and foremost is the ability to perceive that a particular subordinate clause is doing the work of an adverb in the sentence of which it is a part.

After that, it may be useful to identify that adverb-clause as being a a particular kind of adverb-clause; or it may satisfy our grammatical curiosity to do so.

In either event, the detailed classifications provided later in this chapter give the necessary information.

First things first, however. Our starting point is the essential function of adverb-clauses (of *all* adverb-clauses, whatever their particular kind).

We shall then look at the ten different kinds in a carefully-planned sequence, hoping to remove some of the difficulties without omitting any of the essentials.

(b) What does an adverb-clause do?

Put rather obviously, but none the less accurately, it does the work of an adverb; and, as we already know from Section 5.6, an adverb modifies (tells us more about) a verb *or* an adjective *or* another adverb.

REMEMBER

● An adverb-clause is a subordinate clause. Its function is to modify a verb *or* an adjective *or* an adverb in *another* clause.

(c) An adverb-clause modifies a verb in another clause

This function is of first importance. If we start here, we can leave comparatively minor matters until later and sort them out as they arise.

Examples

(The adverb-clauses are printed in italics.)
1 The ferry sailed *when the tide was full.*
2 We installed automatic cameras *where the birds nested.*
3 They lost the election *because the voters did not trust them.*

4 He fitted snow chains *so that the wheels got a grip.*
5 The play flopped *in the way that the critics had predicted.*

In each of these sentences the subordinate clause tells us more about the action denoted by the verb in the other clause. In sentence 1, it tells us *when* the ferry *sailed*; in sentence 2 it tells us *where* we *installed* the cameras; in sentence 3, it tells us *why* (the *reason* why) they *lost* the election; in sentence 4, it tells us the *purpose* for which he *fitted* snow chains; and in sentence 5, it tells us *how* (the *manner* in which) the play *flopped.*

Since each of the sentences we have just been considering is a complex sentence containing only two clauses, the subordinate adverb-clause in each modifies the verb in the main clause. As we know, however, a complex sentence, like a double or a multiple sentence, may contain more than one subordinate clause. In such sentences, the subordinate adverb-clause can modify either the verb in the main clause or a verb in one of the other subordinate clauses.

We have had examples in which the subordinate adverb-clause modifies the verb in another clause by telling us about the time, the place, the reason, the purpose or the manner of the action. (Note that verbs denoting being are modified by adverb-clauses in the same ways.) We can look now at some other kinds of information that an adverb-clause can supply.

It can tell us that what is denoted by the verb in another clause is *conditional upon* the circumstances expressed in the adverb-clause.

Examples

1 I shall be there at six *if I can catch the early bus.*
2 *Unless we accept their price* the deal is off.
3 The attempt will be made tomorrow *provided the weather is fine.*
4 *Supposing it is convenient to you* our representative will call at 10 am.
5 *Had we known earlier* we could have helped.

An adverb-clause can also tell us that what is denoted by a verb in another clause is *exceptional* to the circumstances expressed in the adverb-clause. The adverb-clause *concedes* the statement made in another clause, even though what is stated there is not what would be expected in the circumstances.

Examples

1 *Though I am an optimist,* I expect to lose this match.
2 Read her latest book, *whatever the critics are saying.*

In each of these examples, the statement in the other clause is slightly surprising in view of the circumstances expressed in the adverb-clause. In effect, the adverb-clause says, 'Although you wouldn't expect it to be true, the statement in the other clause must be conceded.'

(d) An adverb-clause modifies an adjective or an adverb in another clause

Examples

1 Our profits were as large *as we could reasonably expect.*
2 He drinks as greedily *as he eats.*

In sentence 1, the adverb-clause modifies the adjective 'large'. It describes the *extent* or *degree* of the largeness of the profits.

In sentence 2, the adverb-clause modifies the adverb 'greedily'. It describes the *extent* or *degree* of the greediness involved.

It is not always easy to decide whether an adverb-clause modifies a verb or an adverb. This difficulty arises when the verb and the adverb that modifies it are so closely linked in meaning that they form a single unit.

Examples

1 The dog barked so fiercely *that the stranger turned away.*
2 She thinks faster *than her opponents do.*

In sentence 1, does the adverb-clause modify the verb 'barked' or the adverb 'fiercely'?

In sentence 2, does the adverb-clause modify the verb 'thinks' or the adverb 'faster'?

It is hard to give a positive answer to those question, but the difficulty does not affect the nature of the subordinate clauses in those two sentences. Each modifies either the verb or an adverb in the other clause. Each is, therefore, an adverb-clause. In any case, common sense tells us that 'barked so fiercely' and 'thinks faster' should be treated as two word *groups*, each of which is modified *as a whole* by an adverb-clause.

The adverb-clause 'that the stranger turned away' tells us the *result* of the dog's barking so fiercely.

The adverb-clause 'than her opponents do' *compares* how fast she thinks with how fast her opponents think.

(e) Identifying adverb-clauses
Now that you are familiar with the general nature of adverb-clauses you should not have much difficulty in identifying them. Proceed as follows:

(i) Is this a subordinate clause?
(ii) With which word (or group of words) in another clause is it most closely associated?

(iii) Is that word a verb? Is it an adjective or an adjective equivalent? Is it an adverb or an adverb equivalent? If it is any one of these three, the clause is a subordinate adverb-clause.

(f) Classification of adverb-clauses

The various kinds of adverb-clauses are listed here, and under each heading you will find examples of words that often introduce each kind. (Such words are called 'subordinating conjunctions' and they will be discussed in Chapter 12.) Do remember that a clause cannot be positively identified by its 'introducer' alone. The word at the beginning of the adverb-clause is often a useful indicator of the kind of clause that follows, but it does not provide proof of identity. That can be found only by recognising the function of the clause in the sentence of which it forms a part.

Adverb-clauses of time
These answer the question *when?*. Often introduced by: after, as, before, since, until, when, whenever, while.

The driver applied the brakes *when he saw the red light.*

Adverb-clauses of place
These answer the question *where?*. Often introduced by: where, wherever, whence, whither.

We bought spares *wherever we could.*

Adverb-clauses of manner
These answer the question *how?*. Often introduced by: as, as if, like.

He finished the marathon *as if it had been a sprint.*

Adverb-clauses of reason or cause
These answer the question *why?*. Often introduced by: as, because, since, that.

The signals faded *because the batteries ran down.*

Adverb-clauses of purpose
These answer the question *for what purpose?*. Often introduced by: in order that, lest, so that, that.

We paid a deposit *so that they reserved the room for us.*

Adverb-clauses of result or consequence
These answer the question *with what result?*. Often introduced by: that, such. . .that, so. . .that.

Scrooge was so mean *that his friends shunned him.*

Adverb-clauses of condition
These answer the question *under what condition(s)?*. Often introduced by: if, in case, on condition that, supposing (that), provided/providing (that), unless, whether.

If I have luck with the papers I shall pass the examination.

Adverb-clauses of concession
These answer the question *even though what?*. Often introduced by: although, even, even if, even though, however, though, whatever, whichever.

She never complained *though the work was hard.*

Adverb-clauses of comparison
These answer the question *compared with what?*. Often introduced by: as, than, such, such as, so, so as.

People will demand a bigger share *than they get now.*

Adverb-clauses of degree or extent
These answer the question *to what degree?*. Often introduced by: as, more, much.

She walked as gracefully *as she danced.*

The distinctions between the different kinds of adverb-clauses are often perfectly clear. For example, clauses of time, place, purpose, reason, result, concession and condition are readily recognised and distinguished. Clauses of manner, comparison and degree are sometimes hard to identify positively, though they are always quite clearly adverb-clauses.

It is never worth spending a lot of time over a knotty and minute problem of identification. It *is* always important to recognise when any particular clause is functioning as an adverb, but it is not often necessary to go further than that. The list of various adverb-clauses is much better used as an aid to the identification of adverb-clauses in general than regarded as a sort of grammatical microscope under which every subordinate clause must be laboriously examined.

Test 43
Answers on page 170.
Identify the adverb-clauses in this passage. State in each case which word in another clause is modified by the adverb-clause.

Though the peasant promised to show them the way through the swamp, the leader of the rebels did not trust him. He made him march where he could watch him closely and, after they had been on the move for an hour, he ordered the old man's right arm to be tied to his stirrup leather. The peasant protested. If they treated him like that, he would not act as their guide. The leader's distrust was so obvious and his anger so great that, though some of them pitied the old man, none of the rebels felt inclined to interfere on his behalf. Their guide must march as their leader decreed. In any case, he was probably as untrustworthy as all the others of his tribe had proved to be.

(g) Clause introducers and clause functions

We have stressed the importance of identifying by function and not by appearance. Do not be misled. Remember that the same word can introduce clauses of different kinds.

Examples

1 We posted guards where the man had been seen.
2 We posted guards at the entrance where the man had been seen.

In example 1, *where the man had been seen* is a subordinate adverb-clause (of place) modifying the verb 'posted'. In example 2, *where the man had been seen* is a subordinate adjective-clause qualifying the noun 'entrance'. Yet the two clauses begin with the same word ('where') and are identical in their wording.

Further examples

1 My grandfather married when he was twenty-one.
2 In the year when he was twenty-one my grandfather married.

The subordinate clause in sentence 1 is an adverb-clause (of time) modifying the verb 'married'. The subordinate clause in sentence 2 is an adjective-clause qualifying the noun 'year'. Yet the two clauses begin with the same word ('when') and are identical in their wording.

Test 44

Answers on page 170.
Identify the subordinate clauses as adverb-clauses or adjective-clauses.

1   We saved hard for several years until we could buy a new car.
2   They then moved to a village where they had relatives.
3   He lived all his life where he was born.
4   That is a shop where you will find some real bargains.
5   After the announcement was made, the guests left quietly.

10.4 NOUN-CLAUSES

(a) Introduction

Noun-clauses are noun equivalents. They do the same work in a sentence as nouns *or* pronouns *or* noun-phrases. Therefore, a noun-clause can function in the following ways: as the subject of a verb; as the object of a verb; as the complement of a verb; as the object of a preposition, as the object of a non-finite verb; as words in apposition to the subject or to the object of a verb.

(b) Noun-clause as the subject of a verb

Examples

1   *That she survived in those conditions* passes belief.
2   *Where he was in the spring of 1970* is still uncertain.
3   *What the minister most feared* now happened.

There are two finite verbs in each of those sentences and, therefore, two clauses; and in each sentence, the noun-clause is the subject of the verb in the second clause.

A complex sentence in which a noun-clause is the subject provides an exception to the rule that a main clause makes sense on its own. Indeed, it is misleading to describe such sentences as having a main clause, for neither clause can make sense without the other:

1   That she survived in those conditions. . .
    . . .passes belief
2   Where he was in the spring of 1970. . .
    . . .is still uncertain
3   What the minister most feared. . .
    . . .now happened

The grammatical structure becomes plain when a noun is substituted for the noun-clause and the resulting sentence is analysed graphically:

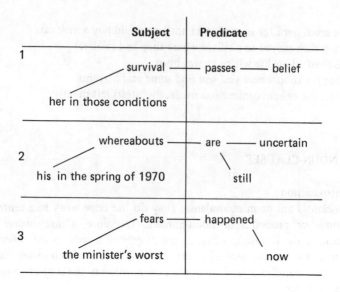

	Subject	Predicate

1 survival ——— passes ——— belief
   her in those conditions

2 whereabouts ——— are ——— uncertain
   his in the spring of 1970   still

3 fears ——— happened
   the minister's worst   now

(c) Noun-clause as the object of a verb

Examples

1 We decided *that we would buy the house.*
2 The repentant children admitted *what they had done.*
3 Astronomers have calculated *when that comet will reappear.*

When a noun-clause functions as the object of a verb the rank of the clauses is not in doubt. In each of the above examples, there is clearly a main clause to which the noun-clause is subordinate.

(d) Noun-clause as the complement of a verb

Examples

1 My theory is *that he forged the will.*
2 A new deal was *what the electors demanded.*
3 The documents will not be *where a casual intruder will find them.*

(e) Noun-clause as the object of a preposition

Examples

1 We cannot provide seats for *all who may come.*
2 Victory depends on *whether we can crack the code.*
3 This society is run by *those who make the most noise.*

When the question *who?* or *what?* is asked after the preposition the noun-clause provides the answer. Thus, the noun-clause is the object of the preposition. The preposition and its noun-clause object function in exactly the same way as a prepositional phrase (see Section 5.7).

(f) Noun-clause as the object of a non-finite verb

A noun-clause that follows either a gerund *or* a participle *or* an infinitive acts as the object of a non-finite verb. When the question *who?* or *what?* is asked after the gerund *or* the participle *or* the infinitive, the answer is supplied by the noun-clause.

Examples

1 (Gerund.) Our rules forbid wearing *whatever members happen to fancy.*
2 (Participle.) The manager heard guests complaining *that their dinner was cold.*
3 (Infinitive.) We had to read it several times to discover *what it meant.*

(g) Noun-clause in apposition to subject or object

Examples

1 The news *that the ship was lost* depressed us all.

In that sentence, the noun-clause *that the ship was lost* and the subject-word 'news' denote exactly the same thing, so they are 'in apposition' to each other (see Section 8.2).

2 We shall abolish the regulation *that applicants must pay a fee.*

In that sentence, the noun-clause *that applicants must pay a fee* and the object-word 'regulation' denote exactly the same thing, so they are in apposition to each other.

Care must be taken to distinguish between a noun-clause in apposition and an adjective-clause.

Examples

1 They received information *that their car had been stolen.*
The subordinate clause does not *qualify* (describe) the noun 'information'. It denotes exactly the same thing as that noun. It is a noun-clause in apposition to the object-word.
2 They received information *that changed their plans.*
The subordinate clause *qualifies* (describes) the noun 'information'. It is an adjective-clause.

Those two examples illustrate another point. When 'that' introduces a noun-clause it is a subordinating conjunction (see Chapter 12). When 'that' introduces an adjective-clause it is a relative pronoun (see Chapter 12). However, 'that' – whether acting as a subordinating conjunction or as a relative pronoun – is frequently omitted. Nevertheless, its 'ghost' is always present in the two constructions.

Examples

1 We thought *(that) he was married.* (Noun-clause, object of verb and introduced by 'understood' subordinating conjunction.)
2 The book *(that) I borrowed from the library* is overdue. (Adjective-clause introduced by 'understood' relative pronoun.)

Test 45
Answers on page 171.
Identify the noun-clauses and describe the function of each.

1 Their supporters still think that they could win the cup.
2 How they are going to do it is not very clear.
3 The directors will not tell anyone what their plans are.
4 Their manager has heard the rumour that his resignation is expected.
5 He has issued a statement denying that he will resign.
6 Everything now depends on who is in control.
7 The journalists want to discover what the facts are.
8 The situation at the ground is not what the club hoped for at the beginning of the season.

Test 46
Answers on page 171.
Identify the subordinate clauses, stating the kind and function of each.

1 When Bunbury first presented himself as a candidate, even his friends were amused.
2 Eventually, the fans realised that their idol had clay feet.
3 Several who were present have assured me that the performance was a great success.
4 When we arrived, the house was deserted except for an old servant who was in a state of shock.
5 You should go to bed now unless you have a good reason for staying up late.

THE ANALYSIS OF COMPLEX, DOUBLE AND MULTIPLE SENTENCES

11.1 METHOD

The graphic method recommended for the analysis of simple sentences is not suited to the analysis of complex, double and multiple sentences. Its basic diagram (see Section 8.3 (g)) provides an instructive visual display of simple sentence structure, but it cannot be stretched to display the structure of a sentence that contains more than one subject and predicate.

A satisfactory method of analysing complex, double and multiple sentences must meet the following requirements:

  (i) Each individual clause in the sentence must be identified.
 (ii) Its kind must be stated.
(iii) Its function in the sentence must be described.
(iv) Its relationship to another clause or other clauses must be described.
 (v) The sentence type must be shown.

The table that follows – a development of the table used in Section 10.2 – meets the requirements just set out. We shall make use of it first to analyse complex sentences. Then we shall apply it to the analysis of double and multiple sentences.

Example

As soon as I arrived in New York, I telephoned my home in England where my wife was waiting anxiously for news.

	Clause	Kind	Function	Link
A	I telephoned my home in England	Main		
a¹	As soon as I arrived in New York	Subordinate adverb-clause (of time)	modifies verb *telephoned* in **A**	As soon as
a²	where my wife was waiting anxiously for news	Subordinate adjective-clause	qualifies noun *home* in **A**	where

Sentence type: complex

Notes

1 The main clause is labelled A.
2 It is placed first in the table, regardless of its position in the sentence.
3 Subordinate clauses are labelled a¹, a², and so on.
4 Linking words are included in the clause to which they belong, but they are also identified separately in the link column of the table.

11.2 PROCEDURE

Whether the sentence to be analysed is complex, double or multiple, a standardised procedure guards against errors and omissions. The following step-by-step approach is recommended:

  (i) Find all the finite verbs.
 (ii) Pick out each separate clause.
(iii) Identify the main clause(s).
 (iv) Identify each subordinate clause.
  (v) Work out what kind of a clause each subordinate clause is by discovering: (a) its function and (b) its relationship to the other clause(s).

11.3 NOTES ON PROCEDURE

(a) Finding the finite verbs

There is one clause for each finite verb in the sentence. A finite verb is a verb that has a subject. Check that the verb *is* finite by finding its subject.

(b) Picking out the separate clauses

Sometimes we have difficulty in deciding where a clause begins and ends. The following hints will help:

(i) Remember that one clause can be embedded in another. For example: 'The criticism that *hurt* him most *came* from friends who, while they *tried* to help him, *shook* his self-confidence.' There are four clauses in that sentence.

(ii) Remember that phrases of all kinds (prepositional, participial, gerundive, infinitive and adverbial) are *parts of clauses*. Each phrase should be included in its own clause in the analysis.

(c) Identifying the main clause(s)

The main clause makes the main statement in a sentence. It can stand alone and make sense without the help of another clause. (The exception to that rule was discussed in Section 10.4(b).) There is one main clause in a complex sentence; there are two in a double sentence and more than two in a multiple sentence.

(d) Identifying the subordinate clause(s)

Unlike a main clause, a subordinate clause cannot make complete sense on its own. It needs help from another clause. Remember, too, that every subordinate clause begins with an introducing/linking word, either expressed or 'understood'. That introducing/linking word is *part of* its subordinate clause and should be included in that clause in the analysis. When the introducing/linking word is 'understood' it should be entered in brackets in the analysis.

(e) Discovering the function and the relationships of a subordinate clause

Find the word (or group of words) in *another* clause with which the subordinate clause is linked or to which it refers. Ask these questions: What part of speech is that word? Does this subordinate clause qualify it or modify it? How does this subordinate clause relate to it structurally?

11.4 WORKED EXAMPLES: COMPLEX SENTENCES

1 Even though the general public seemed indifferent to their cause, the dedicated reformers refused to be silenced when the government turned its full might against them.

Analysis step-by-step

(i) The finite verbs are: 'seemed', 'refused', 'turned'. Their subjects are: 'public', 'reformers', 'government'. There are three finite verbs. There are, therefore, three clauses.

(ii) The clauses are:
    (1) Even though the general public seemed indifferent to their cause
    (2) the dedicated reformers refused to be silenced
    (3) when the government turned its full might against them
(iii) One of those clauses can stand alone and make complete sense without the help of the others: 'the dedicated reformers refused to be silenced'. It is, therefore, the main clause.
(iv) The two other clauses are not independent. Each needs help from another clause to make sense. Each is introduced by a linking word or words: 'Even though. . .'/'when. . .'. They are subordinate clauses.
(v) The subordinate clause 'Even though the general public seemed indifferent to their cause' refers to the verb 'refused' in the main clause. It tells us more about that verb – it modifies it. The action denoted by 'refused' was performed despite the circumstances set out in the subordinate clause. The subordinate clause is an adverb-clause (of concession).

    The subordinate clause 'when the government turned its full might against them' refers to the verb 'refused' in the main clause. It tells us more about that verb – it modifies it. The action denoted by 'refused' was performed when the event described in the subordinate clause took place. The subordinate clause is an adverb-clause (of time).
(vi) In conclusion, the sentence is complex because it has *one* main clause.

Tabular analysis

	Clause	Kind	Function	Link
A	the dedicated reformers refused to be silenced	Main		
a^1	Even though the general public seemed indifferent to their cause	Subordinate adverb-clause (of concession)	modifies verb *refused* in A	Even though
a^2	when the government turned its full might against them	Subordinate adverb-clause (of time)	modifies verb *refused* in A	when

Sentence type: complex

2 After the house went up for sale, we decided that we could not afford to let it go unless we received better offers.

Analysis step-by-step

(i)   The finite verbs are: 'went', 'decided', 'could' (not) 'afford', 'received'. There subjects are: 'house', 'we', 'we', 'we'. There are four finite verbs. There are, therefore, four clauses.

(ii)   The clauses are:

(1) After the house went up for sale

(2) we decided

(3) that we could not afford to let it go

(4) unless we received better offers

(iii)   One of those clauses can stand alone and make complete sense without the help of the others: 'we decided'. It is, therefore, the main clause.

(iv)   The three other clauses are not independent. Each needs help from another clause to make sense. Each is introduced by a linking word: 'After. . .'/'that. . .'/'unless. . .'. They are subordinate clauses.

(v)   The subordinate clause 'After the house went up for sale' refers to the verb 'decided' in the main clause. It tells us more about that verb – it modifies it. The action denoted by 'decided' was performed when the event described in the subordinate clause took place. The subordinate clause is an adverb-clause (of time).

The subordinate clause 'that we could not afford to let it go' is the object of the verb 'decided' in the main clause (decided *what?* 'that we could not afford to let it go'). It is a noun-clause.

The subordinate clause 'unless we received better offers' refers to the verb 'could' (not) 'afford' in the subordinate noun-clause. It tells us more about that verb – it modifies it. It tells us the conditions under which the action denoted by that verb might be or would be performed. It is an adverb-clause (of condition).

(vi) In conclusion, the sentence is complex because it has *one* main clause.

Tabular analysis

	Clause	Kind	Function	Link
A	we decided	Main		
a¹	After the house went up for sale	Subordinate adverb-clause (of time)	modifies verb *decided* in **A**	After
a²	that we could not afford to let it go	Subordinate noun-clause	object of verb *decided* in **A**	that
a³	unless we received better offers	Subordinate adverb-clause (of condition)	modifies verb *could* (not) *afford* in a²	unless

Sentence type: complex

11.5 DOUBLE AND MULTIPLE SENTENCE ANALYSIS

The analysis of sentences containing two or more main clauses does not differ either in aims or in practice from the analysis of sentences containing one main clause. Consequently, the same method and procedure are used.

When you are studying the tabular presentation of the sentences analysed in this section, bear in mind that the information set out in the tables is the result of a step-by-step exploration of grammatical structure. To be sure of understanding the analysis you will probably need to refer back to Sections 11.2, 11.3 and 11.4, where method and procedure are set out in detail.

Analysis, as it is demonstrated here, is not an academic exercise. It is the most practical way of learning how English sentences are built. The English language offers its users a great variety of sentence construction. Sentence analysis teaches us to recognise the resources available and to use them appropriately and correctly.

Successful communication in speech and in writing depends very largely on the communicator's ability to frame the kinds of sentences needed for a particular topic, a particular purpose, and a particular occasion.

Example 1

When I revisited my native village after an absence of many years, the house in which the celebrated eighteenth-century composer lived was still standing but had been greatly altered since I last saw it, and its owner told me that he intended to restore it to its original design if he could find a suitable architect.

	Clause	Kind	Function	Link
A	the house was still standing	Main		
B	but (it) had been greatly altered	Main	co-ordinate with A	but
C	and its owner told me	Main	co-ordinate with A and B	and
a^1	When I revisited my native village after an absence of many years	Subordinate adverb-clause (of time)	modifies verb *was* in A	When
a^2	in which the celebrated eighteenth-century composer lived	Subordinate adjective-clause	qualifies noun *house* in A	in which
b^1	since I last saw it	Subordinate adverb-clause (of time)	modifies verb *had been* in B	since
c^1	that he intended to restore it to its original design	Subordinate noun-clause	object of verb *told* in C	that
c^2	if he could find a suitable architect	Subordinate adverb-clause (of condition)	modifies verb *intended* in c^1	if

Sentence type: multiple

Notes

1 Each main clause is labelled with a different capital letter: A, B, C, and so on.

2 Each main clause after the first is described in the function column as 'co-ordinate' with the others.

3 Subordinate clauses that qualify, or modify, or are in a structural relationship with, a word in main clause A are labelled a^1, a^2, a^3, and so on. Subordinate clauses 'belonging to' main clause B are labelled b^1, b^2, and so on. Subordinate clauses 'belonging to' main clause C are labelled c^1, c^2, and so on.

4 An 'understood' subject-word is supplied in brackets (See '(it)' in main clause B). Whatever part of speech it is and whatever its function, an 'understood' word must be supplied in brackets in its appropriate place in the table.

5 All linking words are shown in the link column; not only the introducing/linking words of the subordinate clauses, but also the co-ordinating conjunctions that link the main clauses. (When co-ordinate subordinate clauses are linked by a co-ordinating conjunction, that conjunction must, of course, be entered in the link column.)

Example 2
The mitigating circumstances that arose from the scientific evidence were taken into account by the court of enquiry, but ignored by the popular press when the scandal became public knowledge.

	Clause	Kind	Function	Link
A	the mitigating circumstances were taken into account by the court of enquiry	Main		
B	but (the) (mitigating) (circumstances) (were) ignored by the popular press	Main	co-ordinate with **A**	but
a¹	that arose from the scientific evidence	Subordinate adjective-clause	qualifies noun *circumstances* in **A**	that
b¹	when the scandal became public knowledge	Subordinate adverb-clause (of time)	modifies verb (*were*) in **B**	when

Sentence type: double

Notes

1 An 'understood' subject-word is supplied, in brackets, *together with* its 'understood' adjective qualifications. See clause B.

2 An 'understood' verb is supplied, in brackets. See clause B.

11.6 TESTS IN ANALYSIS

Test 47

Answers on page 171.

Analyse these sentences into their clauses, stating the kind and function of each clause. Identify the sentence type.

1 I will certainly lend you my car if you want it, but I must warn you that it is not very reliable.

2 This is the place where I sat when I was a schoolboy, forty years ago.

3 Although they begged Jenkins to continue as secretary, he refused because he had a lot of work to do and was very tired.

4 Just after the discovery of the weapons, a magistrate who had been distinguished by his independent spirit and who had taken the deposition of the informer was found murdered.

Test 48

These problems can be solved in more than one way. My suggestions are on page 173.

1 Combine these simple sentences into one double sentence:

Nobody wanted to give me the information. I discovered it by chance. I felt better then.

2 Combine these simple sentences into one complex sentence:

The gang wanted to throw the police off the scent. They abandoned the stolen car. It was left twenty miles away from the scene of the crime.

3 Use this group of words – **that I chose** – in three sentences, so that it functions as: (i) an adjective-clause; (ii) a noun-clause object of a finite verb; (iii) a noun-clause object of a non-finite verb.

Test 49

Suggested answers on page 173.

Write three complex sentences, each containing one example of these constructions:

1 A noun-clause in apposition to the direct object of a transitive verb.

2 An adverb-clause of purpose.

3 Two co-ordinate adjective-clauses.

114

Test 50

Answers on page 173.
Identify the sentence types.

1 He knew all along that his resources were inadequate for the task.

2 Long, long ago, in the earliest dawn of human history, this cave was inhabited by ancient man.

3 All this trouble could have been averted if my warnings had been heeded.

4 His fortune, which was considerable, could not long withstand the demands that he made upon it, and he died in penury.

5 Under-rehearsed as she was, her entrance was mistimed, and the actors on stage were disconcerted by her presence, but they carried on through a botched scene with professional skill.

6 It is not always easy to recognise the various kinds of adverb-clauses, but close attention paid to the function of each clause will solve most problems.

7 Count the finite verbs and you will then find out how many clauses there are.

8 The beggar looked searchingly in my face, whined for alms, but, finding me adamant, withdrew his gaze and concentrated on my soft-hearted companion.

THE PARTS OF SPEECH: A CHAPTER FOR REFERENCE

12.1 INTRODUCTION

In Chapters 5 and 6 we began our study of words in the various classes to which they belong according to the work that they do in a sentence. We saw that the same word can function in one way in one sentence and in a different way in another.

Subsequent chapters demonstrated how the parts of speech are grouped together to form phrases, which themselves lock into place in simple sentences and in clauses. Then we examined clauses as the constituent parts of complex, double and multiple sentences.

All the way through, we have emphasised that the purpose of grammatical study is to increase our understanding of, and skill in, sentence construction. We study words as parts of speech solely to explore their function in phrases, in clauses and - finally - in sentences of all kinds.

The fact that the parts of speech are the working parts of sentences is now thoroughly established, so we shall not make the mistake of isolating them from their living environment.

The definitions and classifications provided in this chapter complete our account of technical terms and concepts, many of which we have met already. Details are filled in here, not for their own sake, but because they are useful additions to the grammatical vocabulary needed when describing and analysing word behaviour.

The subject matter of this chapter is not a collection of facts to be memorised. It is designed for *use* when you are examining the grammatical patterns of English sentences. Reference to it will often help you to give an accurate and economical description of those structures.

Knowing the contents of this chapter by heart would add little to the grammatical insights that the earlier chapters have provided. Used properly, however, the information given here will help you to make explicit (either to yourself or to others) your perception of the ways in which words work in the sentences to which they belong.

The chapter is arranged in the order suggested by the list of 'word families' given in Section 5.10. At that stage, we had not studied the relationships that are set up as words perform their various grammatical functions, but now, with our work on phrases, clauses and sentences complete, those 'family ties' provide a natural sequence in which to present the information.

Finally, do not be surprised when you find that some of the items listed are quickly dismissed as being of no practical use. Some grammatical terms and concepts taught in the past have nothing like the importance once assigned to them. (Examples are 'gender' and 'dative case', which have very little to do with the behaviour of the English language.) Such out-of-date notions are listed here because they still clutter up much that is talked and written about English grammar. They are still bandied about, so you need to know them. You also need to know not to trouble your head with them.

12.2 NOUNS

(a) Definition
A noun is a 'naming word'. It names: a person (Jane); a place (London); a non-material thing (sweetness, justice, speed, compassion); a material thing (chair).

(b) Kinds of nouns
Proper nouns name particular people, places, things: Shakespeare, Africa, the United Nations. Proper nouns, when written, always begin with a capital letter.

Abstract nouns name non-material things; qualities, states, concepts that exist only in our minds: happiness, beauty, mercy, sorrow.

Collective nouns name groups or collections of people or things, regarded as a whole: team, crew, fleet.

Common nouns name members of a class of people or things who share the name in common with all the other members of their class: woman, farmer, book.

(c) Number
A noun is either singular or plural, according to whether it names one or more than one person, place, idea or thing.

The plural of a noun is usually formed by adding $-s$ or $-es$ to its singular form: boy/boys; church/churches. There are exceptions (baby/babies; hero/heroes, for example), many of which you will know. Difficulties with the plural forms of nouns are matters of spelling rather than grammar and should be solved by reference to a spelling book or dictionary.

Number plays an important part in grammar because of the rules of agreement (subject/verb; pronoun/antecedent). The point will be dealt with in Chapter 13.

(d) Person

Nouns are always in the 3rd person, either singular or plural. See Section 12.3 for a full treatment of person.

(e) Case

Except in the genitive case, nouns in English do not change their forms to indicate what case they are in. Consequently, the study of case is simpler for the student of English than it is for the student of the 'inflected' languages, such as German, in which case determines noun-forms.

These are the essential facts about the cases of nouns in English (with very brief notes on the non-essential items mentioned in Section 12.1).

Nominative
(i) The case of the subject-word in a clause or a sentence.

That *girl* will be late.

(ii) The case of a noun used predicatively to refer to the subject of a clause or a sentence.

She was a good *actress.*

Vocative
The case of the person or thing addressed.

Betty, I want to see you.

The vocative case is of no importance whatever in English. You will now know what the term means if you come across it. Apart from that, you can ignore it.

Accusative
(i) The case of the direct object-word in a clause or a sentence.

He is preparing *supper.*

(ii) The case of a noun used predicatively to refer to the direct object-word.

They elected her *captain.*

(iii) The case of a noun that is the object of a preposition.

The horse got the bit between its *teeth.*

(iv)   The case of a noun that is the object of a non-finite verb.

Picking *strawberries* is hard work.
He was desperate to win that *game*.

It is important to identify nouns in the accusative case when analysing clauses and sentences because the accusative is essentially the case of the object.

Genitive
The case of possession, and very important because it determines noun forms. A noun in the genitive case must signal its case by its form. Singular nouns use different signals from those used by plural nouns.

(i)   Singular noun adds *'s* to signal that it is genitive.

My *daughter's* school is in Newport Road.

(ii)   Plural noun ending in *s* adds ' to signal that it is genitive.

My *daughters'* school gave them a good education.

(iii)   Plural noun not ending in *s* adds *'s* to signal that it is genitive.

The *women's* co-operative was a success.

(v)   Singular noun ending in *s* adds either ' or *'s* to signal that it is genitive. The choice is determined by the *sound*. For example, in the genitive case, we can use either *Dickens'* or *Dickens's*. There would be few objections to the sound of *Dickens's novels*, but we might think that *Dickens's slippers* made a horrible hissing noise. Similarly, *Ulysses' bow* would sound better than *Ulysses's bow*. What we must *never* do is write *Dicken's novels* or *Keat's poems*. Their names were *Dickens* and *Keats*, not 'Dicken' and 'Keat'.

Dative
The case of the indirect object-word.

We gave the *beggar* a meal.

The dative case is of no practical importance whatever in English, though you will sometimes hear it mentioned as if it mattered.

To sum up: the cases that matter are the nominative, the accusative and the genitive. You need not bother about the others. (We have not even mentioned 'the ablative', which was once much loved by grammarians who tried to force Latin patterns on the English language.)

(f) Gender
The English language long ago lost the concept of 'grammatical gender' that features so prominently in many other languages. In Latin, French

and German, for example, nouns are classified as masculine, feminine and neuter; and that classification determines their 'inflexions' (changes in noun-forms). Classification by gender is irrelevant to English grammar.

12.3 PRONOUNS

(a) Definition
A pronoun is a word that stands for/in place of a noun. It can stand in place of a noun already used, for example: The tourists hired a guide *who* showed *them* round the town. It can stand for a noun not explicitly named, for example: Farmers are always complaining about *it*.

(b) Kinds of pronouns
Personal pronouns
Here is the complete list showing the changes of word-form that personal pronouns make to signal person, number and case.

Person	Number	Nominative	Accusative	Genitive
1st	singular	I	me	mine
2nd	singular	you	you	yours
3rd	singular	he/she/it	him/her/it	his/hers/its
1st	plural	we	us	our
2nd	plural	you	you	yours
3rd	plural	they	them	theirs

Possessive pronouns
They are as listed under the genitive case heading in the table of personal pronouns. The possessive pronouns are personal pronouns in the genitive case. Although they are in the genitive case, the possessive pronouns – unlike nouns – do *not* signal possession with an apostrophe.

Emphasising pronouns
These are: (1st person) myself/ourselves, (2nd person) yourself/yourselves, (3rd person) himself/herself/itself/themselves.

Examples
His parents died young, but he *himself* lived to a ripe old age.
After saving the first swimmer, the lifeguards *themselves* got into danger.

Reflexive pronouns

These have the same form as the emphasising pronouns but they function in a different way. They are used: (i) as the object of a transitive verb; (ii) as the object of a preposition.

Examples

(i) The directors ruined *themselves*.
(ii) She made a great name for *herself*.

The examples illustrate the fact that reflexive pronouns always denote the same person or thing as the subject.

Demonstrative pronouns

They are: this; that; these; those; same; such. They are called *demonstrative* because they 'point out' the person or thing to which they refer.

This is a mistake.
That is a shame.
Offered a selection, we chose the *same*.

Same must always be preceded by the definite article when it is used as a demonstrative pronoun.

Interrogative pronouns

They are: who; whose; whom; which; what. They are used in asking questions.

Who designed this building?
Whom did you see?

You will find more information about *who/whom* in Chapter 13.

Relative pronouns

They are: who; whom; whose, which; that. Relative pronouns are introducing/linking words. They often introduce a subordinate adjective-clause and they *relate* to an *antecedent*. That is why they are called *relative* pronouns. The appropriate relative pronoun is selected according to these rules: *who* and *whom* relate to persons; *which* relates to things; *that* relates to either persons or things.

Examples

He is the only person *who* knows about this.
He is the only person *whom* I have told about this.
This is the actor about *whom* the critics were so enthusiastic.
The policeman cautioned the motorist *whose* car was badly parked.
My uncle, on *whose* advice I relied, was my only relative.
The new model *that* (or *which*) has just arrived will suit you.
The late arrivals are the people *that* cause most trouble.

Sometimes *what* functions as a compound relative pronoun. It is then the equivalent of 'that which'. Here is an example: I cannot understand *what* you are saying.

The correct use of relative pronouns is the subject of a special section of Chapter 13.

Pronouns of number or quantity

Examples

We have *one* left.
Give me a *few*.
He did *much* for them.
Several are missing.

The following words are also often used as pronouns of number or quantity; each, either, neither, anybody, anything, everyone, everything.

12.4 ADJECTIVES

(a) Definition
Adjectives tell us more about (qualify) nouns and pronouns. Many words can be either adjectives or pronouns, according to their function in a given sentence. Check that a word *is* an adjective by identifying the noun or pronoun that it qualifies. Remember that a pronoun does *not* qualify: it stands for or in place of.

(b) Kinds of adjectives
Descriptive adjectives
These qualify nouns by describing some quality or attribute attaching to the person or thing denoted by the noun.

Examples
red apples; *deep* pool, *kind* person; *twinkling* stars.

The old name for an adjective closely attached to a noun in this descriptive manner was *epithet.*

Descriptive adjectives generally precede the noun that they qualify, but they are often separated from it and used predicatively: The crops are *ripe.* He was always *anxious.*

Possessive adjectives
These are: (1st person) my/our; (2nd person) your/your; (3rd person) his/her/its/their.

Possessive adjectives must not be confused with possessive pronouns. Possessive adjectives always qualify a noun or pronoun. Possessive pronouns do not. *And* they have different forms.

Possessive adjectives	Possessive pronouns
That is *her* writing.	Can you recognise *hers*?
My pen is leaking.	Try *mine*.
Do you know *our* house?	Is it near to *ours*?

Demonstrative adjectives
Like demonstrative pronouns, they 'point out'. They are: this, these, that, those, such, same.

Examples
I should like one of the *same* shape.
This question floored a lot of the candidates.
Are *those* melons ripe?

Remember that both *a/an* and *the* are, strictly speaking, demonstrative adjectives, though they are always identified by their special names: the 'indefinite article' and the 'definite article'.

Relative adjectives
They are: *which* and *what*. They introduce relative clauses.

Examples

You can take *which* route you like.
I gave him *what* money I could spare.

Interrogative adjectives
They are: which, what, whose.

Examples

Which suit shall I wear?
What choice have I?
Whose tie is this?

Adjectives of number or quantity
They include all the numerals (cardinal and ordinal). They also include many words that can also be pronouns, for example: some, both, certain, all, few, much, each.

Examples

The *third* horse was my choice.
Four other horses finished the race.
You will not have *much* food to spare.

(c) Comparison of adjectives

Adjectives have three 'degrees of comparison': positive; comparative; superlative.

Examples

His grandfather is a *tall* man. (*positive* degree)
His father is *taller* than his grandfather. (*comparative* degree)
He is the *tallest* of the three men. (*superlative* degree)
The superlative degree should be used only when more than two people or things are being compared.

The degrees of comparison of adjectives are formed in two ways.

1 By adding -*er* and -*est* to the positive form. Sometimes a change of spelling is also required:

Positive	Comparative	Superlative
big	bigger	biggest
happy	happier	happiest
rich	richer	richest
sad	sadder	saddest
small	smaller	smallest

2 By using *more* and *most* with the positive form:

Positive	Comparative	Superlative
ambitious	more ambitious	most ambitious
doubtful	more doubtful	most doubtful
positive	more positive	most positive.

There is no clear-cut rule about the method to be used when forming the degrees of comparison. The general guideline to be used is as follows. The comparative and superlative forms of longer words are made with 'more' and 'most', not with -*er* and -*est*. (We do not use 'ambitiouser' or 'positivest', for example.) Shorter words are usually given the -*er* and -*est* endings in their comparative and superlative forms. (However, we do use 'most pretty' as well as 'prettiest'; and there are many other examples of acceptable alternatives.) Idiom is a better guide than grammar in this respect.

The *irregular* forms, on the other hand, offer us no choice. (We cannot use 'mucher' or 'muchest'; 'badder' or 'baddest'. There are no such forms in English.)

The *irregular degrees of comparison* are:

Positive	*Comparative*	*Superlative*
bad	worse	worst
good	better	best
little	less	least
many	more	most
much	more	most

REMEMBER No choice with those.

12.5 VERBS

(a) Definition
A verb is a word that denotes action or being. Its function in a sentence is to make a statement about the subject of that sentence.

Examples

The director *signed* the letter.
The contractors *demolished* the building.
Retribution *followed* swiftly.
His son *became* famous.
You *are* the boss.

    A verb may consist of more than one word, and other words may come in between the various components of the compound verb.

Examples

I *was watching* tennis.
Jones *has been offered* a new job.
They *will* soon *realise* their mistake.
The book *has* at last *been published*.

(b) Person and number
A verb agrees with its subject in person and in number. This grammatical rule, to which there are no exceptions, is not always obvious, because English verbs do not often change their form to signal person and number. Nearly all English verbs make just one change to indicate person and number: the *-s* inflexion that signals 3rd person singular.

    The verb *to be* does, however, make form changes to signal person and number: I am; you are; he/she/it is; I was; you were; he/she/it was.

Examples of subject/verb agreement
I *drive* to the station. (1st person singular)
She *drives* to the station. (3rd person singular)
They *drive* to the station. (3rd person plural)
I *was driving* to the station. (1st person singular)
We *were driving* to the station. (1st person plural)
The bottles *were* on the doorstep. (3rd person plural)
The crate of bottles *was* on the doorstep. (3rd person singular)

Problems of subject/verb agreement will be dealt with in Chapter 13.

(c) Transitive and intransitive verbs

A transitive verb has a direct object. The action denoted by a transitive verb is 'carried across' from the doer of the action (the subject) to the receiver of the action (the direct object).

Examples
The rain *revived* the wilting shrubs.
Brutus *stabbed* Caesar.
The man *chased* the dog.
The dog *chased* the man.

An intransitive verb does not have a direct object. The action denoted by an intransitive verb 'stays with' the subject: it is not carried across to a receiver. An intransitive verb can make a complete predicate on its own; or the predicate may consist of the intransitive verb plus modifications of that verb.

Examples
The quartz crystal *used* in a watch vibrates.
The choir *sang* badly that morning.

Many verbs can be used either transitively or intransitively.

Examples
The choir *sang* an anthem. ('sang' is used transitively)
The choir *sang* badly. ('sang' is used intransitively)
He *hit* his opponent hard in the second round. ('hit' is used transitively)
He *hit* hard in the second round. ('hit' is used intransitively)

(d) Verbs of incomplete predication

Many verbs used intransitively can form a predicate on their own. ('He ran'. 'The vessel sank'. 'The car swerved'.) A few verbs cannot do that. The chief examples are: the verb *to be* (in all its forms); *to become*; *to seem*. Those verbs cannot complete their predicates without help. Complements (predicative words) must be supplied to make a complete predicative statement. That is why they are called 'verbs of incomplete predication'.

Examples

My son *became*. . .
The situation *seems*. . .
We *were*. . .

In each of these examples, the sense is incomplete. Complements (predicative words) must be supplied to make a complete statement about the subject.

(e) Non-finite verbs

A finite verb is a verb with a subject. It is 'limited' by its subject, with which it must agree in person and in number. In a clause or a sentence, a finite verb forms the predicate or part of the predicate.

A non-finite verb has no subject. It is not 'limited'. It may function in either the subject or in the predicate of a clause or a sentence.

There are four kinds of non-finite verbs. They are: the infinitive; the gerund; the present participle; the past participle.

I. *The infinitive*

The infinitive begins with 'to': *to see*, *to wait*, and so on. It functions: (i) as a verb-noun; (ii) as an adverb modifying a verb; (iii) as an adverb modifying an adjective; (iv) as an adjective qualifying a noun.

(i) *The infinitive as a verb-noun*

As a verb-noun, the infinitive may be the subject, *or* the direct object, *or* the complement of a verb in a clause or a sentence.

Examples

Infinitive as *subject*: *To read* poetry gives me special pleasure.
Infinitive as *direct object*: They agreed *to discuss* our proposals.
Infinitive as *complement*: Her dream is *to become* an actress.

(ii) *The infinitive as an adverb modifying a verb*

This very common construction is sometimes called 'the infinitive of purpose'.

Example

They walked home *to save* the bus fare.

(iii) *The infinitive as an adverb modifying an adjective*

Example

His appeal seems certain *to be rejected*.

(iv) The infinitive as an adjective qualifying a noun

Example
Have you any fuel *to spare*

2 *The gerund*

The gerund is a verb-noun. It usually ends in *-ing* (see Section 12.5 (g)).
The gerund functions: (i) as subject; (ii) as direct object; (iii) as complement; (iv) as the object of a preposition.

(i) Gerund as subject

Example
In that firm's present state, *balancing* the books will not be easy.

(ii) Gerund as direct object

Example
He hated *wasting* his money.

(iii) Gerund as complement

Example
Her favourite pastime is *reading.*

(iv) Gerund as object of a preposition

Example
The student annoyed the lecturer by *asking* too many questions.

'You may accompany me.'
a gerund permits an adjective to be its qualifier

Like any other noun, the gerund as verb-noun can be qualified by adjectives. For example: 'Quiet *talking* after lights-out is permitted.' 'This excellent *fishing* is a major attraction.' In such uses, the noun function of the gerund is so dominant that it may be regarded simply as a noun. Like many nouns, the gerund can function as an adjective. For example: 'the *London* train' (noun as adjective); 'walking-stick' (gerund as verb-noun-adjective: 'stick *for* walking').

The present participle
Like the gerund, the present participle is an -*ing* form of the verb, but it functions as an adjective.

The present participle: (i) qualifies a noun or a pronoun; (ii) introduces an adjective-phrase qualifying a noun or a pronoun; (iii) forms part of an 'absolute construction'; (iv) combines with auxiliary verbs to form the continuous tenses (see Section 12.5 (g)).

(i) Present participle qualifying a noun or a pronoun

Examples
The surgeon's report was *encouraging*.
A *worrying* time now ended.

In such uses, the present participle may be regarded simply as a descriptive adjective.

(ii) Present participle introducing an adjective-phrase

Example
Passing all the tests with ease, the candidate impressed the selectors.

See Section 13.5 (d).

(iii) Present participle forming part of an absolute construction

Example
Conditions *being* favourable, we shall start tomorrow.
The judge *consenting*, the trial will be postponed.

An absolute construction is so called because it has no grammatical bonds with the rest of the sentence. It is 'free' ('absolute'). It is an adverb equivalent. See Section 13.5 (e).

(iv) Present participle in continuous tenses

Examples
The train is *leaving*. The train was *leaving*. The train will be *leaving*.

The past participle
Like the present participle, the past participle is a verb-adjective. Unlike

the present participle (which always has the -*ing* termination) the past participle takes several forms – see Section 7.2 (d).

The past participle: (i) qualifies a noun or a pronoun; (ii) introduces an adjective-phrase qualifying a noun or a pronoun; (iii) forms part of an absolute construction – see Section 13.5 (e); (iv) combines with auxiliary verbs to form the passive voice (see Section 12.5 (f)) and certain past tenses (see Section 12.5 (g)).

(i) Past participle qualifying a noun or a pronoun

Examples
Their *defeated* champion lost his title.
We found the bathroom pipes *frozen*.

In such uses, the adjective function of the past participle is so dominant that it may be regarded simply as a descriptive adjective.

(ii) Past participle introducing an adjective-phrase

Examples
Infuriated by the backbenchers' revolt, the prime minister gave way.
Having cleared my desk I went on holiday.
See Section 13.5 (d).

(iii) Past participle in an absolute construction

Examples
The prototype *having been* thoroughly *tested*, the engineers had solid grounds for their optimism.

(iv) Past participle in voice and tense forms

Examples
That cloak *was worn* by Irving when he played Hamlet. (Passive voice)
I *had* often *seen* her without guessing her true identity. (Past perfect tense)

(f) Voice – active and passive
Verbs have two 'voices': active and passive. The active voice indicates that the subject of the verb acts. The passive voice indicates that the subject of the verb is acted upon.

Examples
The head gardener *planted* the rare shrub. (Active voice)
The rare shrub *was planted* by the head gardener. (Passive voice)

The subject of the verb in the active construction 'The head gardener' performs the action. The subject of the verb in the passive construction 'the rare shrub' is acted upon. It undergoes or receives the action. Note, too, that the direct object of the verb in the active voice becomes the subject of the verb in the passive voice.

A verb in the active voice shows that the action it denotes is performed by the subject.

A verb in the passive voice shows that the action it denotes is performed upon the subject. Passive means 'suffering', so - in traditional grammatical terms - the subject 'suffers' the action denoted by a verb in the passive voice. 'Suffers' is not always a sensible description of how the action affects the subject. The following suggestions fit a wider range of circumstances.

When the verb is in the passive voice, the subject of that verb receives/ undergoes/experiences the action denoted by the verb.

Examples of verbs in the passive voice
The audience *was delighted* by the play.

Ruritania *was overwhelmed* by her enemies.

That comet *will be seen* again in exactly one hundred years from now.

The passive voice is usually formed by combining the past participle with the appropriate form of the verb *to be*, as in the examples just given: 'was' + 'delighted'; 'was' + 'overwhelmed'; 'will be' + 'seen'.

The passive voice may also be formed by combining the past participle with the appropriate form of the verb *to get*. For example: 'They *got caught* at the frontier'.

(g) Tense
Tense means 'time'. The tense of a verb indicates whether the action (or the state of being) denoted by the verb takes place in the present, took place in the past or will take place in the future.

Tense also indicates whether the action denoted by the verb is simple, continuous or completed. The term *imperfect* (meaning 'not finished', 'still going on') is often used as a synonym for 'continuous'. The term *perfect* (meaning 'finished', 'over') is more often used than 'completed'.

Simple tenses
A simple tense is a tense 'without complications'. It denotes present, past or future in a direct way. It makes a simple statement about the time of the action

'*I ride*'; '*he rides*' are the 1st and 3rd person singular of the present simple tense of the verb *to ride*.

'*I rode*'; '*he rode*' are the 1st and 3rd person singular of the past simple tense.

'*I shall ride*'; '*he will ride*' are the 1st and 3rd person singular of the future simple tense.

Continuous tenses

The continuous tenses, indicating that an action is, was or will be continuing, are formed by combining the auxiliary verb *to be* with the present participle.

'*I am riding*'; '*he is riding*' are the 1st and 3rd person singular of the present continuous tense of the verb *to ride*.

'*I was riding*'; '*he was riding*' are the 1st and 3rd person singular of the past continuous tense.

'*I shall be riding*'; '*he will be riding*' are the 1st and 3rd person singular of the future continuous tense.

Perfect tenses

The perfect tenses, indicating that an action is, was or will be completed (finished, over), are formed by combining the auxiliary verb *to have* with the past participle.

'*I have ridden*'; '*he has ridden*' are the 1st and 3rd person singular of the present perfect tense of the verb *to ride*.

'*I had ridden*'; '*he had ridden*' are the 1st and 3rd person singular of the past perfect tense.

'*I shall have ridden*'; '*he will have ridden*' are the 1st and 3rd person singular of the future perfect tense.

The future in the past tense

This tense denotes an action that, at a point in past time, still lay in the future.

Examples

I told them that I *should write* the letter the next day.

The tense of the verb *told* shows that the event occurred in the past. At that moment in the past, the action of writing the letter lay in the future. I had not yet written the letter. I was going to write it.

She hoped that she *would be invited* to their party.

The tense of the verb *hoped* indicates past time. At that moment in the past, she had not been invited to their party. The desired event lay in the future.

The government calculated that oil revenues *would have been exhausted* before the next election took place.

The tense of the verb *calculated* indicates past time. At that moment in the past, the oil revenues had not been exhausted. That eventuality lay in the future. (The verb *would have been exhausted* is in the passive voice.)

Like all the other tenses, the future in the past has simple, continuous and perfect forms.

'*I should ride*'; '*he would ride*' are the 1st and 3rd person singular of the future simple in the past tense of the verb *to ride*.

'*I should be riding*'; '*he would be riding*' are the 1st and 3rd person singular of the future continuous in the past tense.

'*I should have ridden*'; '*he would have ridden*' are the 1st and 3rd person singular of the future perfect in the past tense.

(h) Check-list of tenses

Example — the verb 'to ride' (active voice)

Present simple tense
I ride; you ride; he/she/it rides
we ride; you ride; they ride

Past simple tense
I rode; you rode; he/she/it rode
we rode; you rode; they rode

Future simple tense
I shall ride; you will ride; he/she/it will ride
we shall ride; you will ride; they will ride

Future simple in the past tense
I should ride; you would ride; he/she/it would ride
we should ride; you would ride; they would ride

Present continuous tense
I am riding; you are riding; he/she/it is riding
we are riding; you are riding; they are riding

Past continuous tense
I was riding; you were riding; he/she/it was riding
we were riding; you were riding; they were riding

Future continuous tense
I shall be riding; you will be riding; he/she/it will be riding
we shall be riding; you will be riding; they will be riding

Future continuous in the past tense
I should be riding; you would be riding; he/she/it would be riding
we should be riding; you would be riding; they would be riding

Present perfect tense
I have ridden; you have ridden; he/she/it has ridden
we have ridden; you have ridden; they have ridden

Past perfect tense
I had ridden; you had ridden; he/she/it had ridden
we had ridden; you had ridden; they had ridden

Future perfect tense
I shall have ridden; you will have ridden; he/she/it will have ridden
we shall have ridden; you will have ridden; they will have ridden

Future perfect in the past tense
I should have ridden; you would have ridden; he/she/it would have ridden
we should have ridden; you would have ridden; they would have ridden

Notes
1 The present simple tense is used in several ways:
(i) With adverb modifications to refer to future times.

We *start* our holidays next week.

(ii) To express habitual action.

He *pays* his debts promptly.

He has done so in the past, so we may suppose that he does so now and
will do so in the future. Compare the present continuous tense: 'He *is
paying* his debts promptly', meaning that the action is taking place at the
time that the statement is made.
(iii) To express a general truth, or what is held to be a general truth.

Suppressed aggression *is* a cause of depression.

(iv) In the narration of past events as if they were happening before the
reader's eyes or in the hearer's presence. The present simple tense is used
in this way to produce a vivid effect and it is called the 'historic present'.

2 'Used to' expresses habitual action in past time.

She *used to go* to the theatre every week.

3 Future time is often indicated by the present continuous tense of the
verb *to go* combined with an infinitive.

We are *going to buy* a new chair.

'About to' is used for the same purpose, but with the implication of
immediate action.

They are *about to close* the shop.

4 As the check-list of tenses showed, 'shall' and 'will' are used to form the
future tenses; 'should' and 'would' are used to form the future in the past
tenses. They are auxiliary verbs, helping other verbs to form those tenses.

The rules are:
1st person singular and plural: shall and should
2nd and 3rd person singular and plural: will and would

Examples

I *shall stay* in Paris. (1st person singular)
You *will stay* in Paris. (2nd person singular or plural)
We said that we *should take* a taxi. (1st person plural)
They said that they *would take* a taxi. (3rd person plural)

Nowadays, there is general ignorance of the correct use of shall/will and should/would. That ignorance impairs linguistic precision. The rules should be known – and kept.

5 Determination, intention, promise and threat are expressed by will/shall and would/should. In such uses, however, those verbs are not auxiliaries. They are verbs of full meaning, expressing more than futurity.

The rules (the reverse of those for expressing futurity) are:
1st person singular and plural: will and would
2nd and 3rd person singular and plural: shall and should

Compare these examples

I *shall* post this letter. (Future)
I *will* post this letter. (Determination or intention)
You *will* be rewarded. (Future)
You *shall* be rewarded. (Promise or intention)
I *shall* resign (Future) and nobody *will* stop me. (Future)
I *will* resign (Determination) and nobody *shall* stop me. (Determination)
We said that, whatever the cost, we *would* pay. (Intention)
We have told them that we *shall* pay tomorrow. (Future)

(i) Principal parts

The present tense, the past tense, and the past participle are called the 'principle parts' of a verb. There is a sense in which the present participle is also a principal part, for it combines with the verb *to be* to form the continuous tenses. But, since the present participle of every verb ends with *-ing*, its form gives no difficulty and it is not, therefore, included in the list of principal parts.

The past participle is formed from the present tense in various ways:

(i) By adding *-ed*; *-d*; *-t*; *-en*; *-n* or *-ne*, with or without vowel changes.

Examples

talk/talked; sell/sold; seek/sought; sleep/slept; beat/beaten; know/known; bear/borne.

(ii) By change of vowel(s) only.

Examples
bind/bound; ring/rung; sing/sung

(iii) With no change.

Examples
hit/hit; put/put; set/set

In many verbs, the past participle and the past tense have the same form. In some, they are different. It is this variety of formation, in addition to the several kinds noted already, that makes it important to know the principal parts.

Examples

Present tense	Past tense	Past participle
break	broke	broken
dare	dared	dared
sing	sang	sung
take	took	taken
ride	rode	ridden
write	wrote	written

(j) Mood
There are four 'moods': the indicative; the imperative; the infinitive; the subjunctive.

Indicative
The mood of a verb that states a fact or asks a question.

He *closed* the door.
Has he *closed* the door?

Imperative
The mood of a verb that expresses a command, a request, a wish. A verb in the imperative mood is always in the 2nd person because its subject is always 'you'.

Shut the door.
Please *shut* the door.

Infinitive
The mood of a verb that expresses a general statement with no reference to a subject of its own. It functions as a noun equivalent. It may be in the active or the passive voice and in the present or cŏntinuous tenses. It does not occur in the future tense.

To be asked for a donation irritated me.
Her mistake was *to have been seen* in his company.

Subjunctive

The mood of a verb that expresses a wish, a supposition, a condition. a doubt. It is little used in modern English. In any case, since the form of the subjunctive of most verbs is the same as the form of the indicative, the question of its use is seldom of any concern.

The only uses worth noting are these. The subjunctive mood of the verb *to be* in conditional or suppositional clauses expressing a condition or supposition that cannot be (or is very unlikely to be) fulfilled.

If I *were* you I should demand a refund.
She would make a marvellous Juliet if she *were* twenty years younger.

Its use is also apparent in a noun-clause following a 'wishing' verb.

I wish I *were* anywhere but here.

Those lingering uses of a signalled subjunctive mood are themselves disappearing from modern English, and 'mood', as a whole, is a concept of little practical significance to users of the English language.

(k) Phrasal verbs

The 'phrasal verb' plays an important part in English grammar. English verbs are frequently compounded with another word which is so much a part of their meaning that common sense demands that the verb and its 'companion' should be regarded as a grammatical entity.

Examples

to make up; to put down; to take in; to take off; to switch on – and hundreds more, used as the need arises.

The 'companion words' (up, down, in, off, on) look like prepositions, but it does not make grammatical sense to treat them as such.

The sense of 'They switched on the hall lights' is not 'They/switched/on the hall lights'. The sense is 'They/switched on/the hall lights.' In other words, 'switched on' is a verb used transitively. Its direct object is 'the hall lights'.

In so far as it can be considered apart from the verb, the 'companion word' in a phrasal verb has the function of an adverb. But the grammatical reality is that in a phrasal verb, the 'verb element' and the 'adverb element' are fused into one verb, which may be used transitively or intransitively.
He took off his hat. (Transitive)
They slept in that morning. (Intransitive)

The elements of a phrasal verb are often separated by other parts of speech.

She *took* everyone *in* with her plausible tales.
Their conciliatory policies soon *won* the opposition *over*.

12.6 ADVERBS

An adverb modifies a verb, an adjective or another adverb.

Examples
1 We arrived *early*. (The adverb modifies the verb 'arrived'.)
2 These flowers are *almost* dead. (The adverb modifies the adjective 'dead'.)
3 He talks *so* fast that I cannot understand him. (The adverb modifies the adverb 'fast'.)

Adverbs are classified as: 'simple' 'interrogative' or 'relative'.

(a) Simple adverbs
These indicate: time, place, manner, quantity (extent or degree), number.

Examples
1 The plane landed *late*. (time)
2 It touched down *there*. (place)
3 It came in *slowly*. (manner)
4 The weather was *extremely* bad. (degree)
5 The pilot *twice* tried to land. (number)

(b) Interrogative adverbs
When used as a question-introducer, an adverb modifies a verb by asking: *how?* (manner); *when?* (time); *where?* (place); *why?* (reason).

Examples
1 *How* can we get out of that invitation?
2 *When* are you expecting them?
3 *Where* shall we go?
4 *Why* does this engine run so hot?

(c) Relative adverbs
(i) They function as introducing/linking words which join subordinate adjective-clauses to main clauses. Like relative pronouns, they have an antecedent, which must be clearly identifiable (see Chapter 13).

Examples
1 I have been to Dove Cottage *where* Wordsworth lived.

The relative adverb introduces a subordinate adjective-clause qualifying its antecedent, the (proper) noun 'Dove Cottage'.

2 April is the month *when* showers are most likely.

The relative adverb introduces a subordinate adjective-clause qualifying its antecedent, the noun 'month'.

(ii) They function as introducing/linking words which join subordinate adverb-clauses to main clauses.

Examples

1 We were delighted *when* their letter arrived.

The relative adverb introduces a subordinate adverb-clause of time modifying the verb 'were'.

2 They gave a party *after* the play ended.

The relative adverb introduces a subordinate adverb-clause of time modifying the verb 'gave'.

(iii) They function as introducing/linking words which join subordinate noun-clauses to main clauses.

Examples

1 Do you know *where* the Smiths live?

The relative adverb introduces a subordinate noun-clause, object of the verb 'know'.

2 *Why* he got so angry is not important.

The relative adverb introduces a subordinate noun-clause, subject of the verb 'is'.

(d) Comparison of adverbs

Like adjectives, adverbs form their degrees of comparison in one of two ways. Some add *-er* to form the comparative and *-est* to form the superlative. Others are preceded by 'more' in the comparative and by 'most' in the superlative.

Examples

soon   sooner   soonest
firmly   more firmly   most firmly

The chief irregular forms are:

badly   worse   worst
far   farther   farthest
far   further   furthest
little   less   least
much   more   most
well   better   best

12.7 PREPOSITIONS

A preposition is a 'relating' word. It relates *either* a noun or a pronoun *or* a noun equivalent to another word. That other word may be: (i) a noun; (ii) a verb; (iii) an adjective.

We had a room at the old hotel. (Preposition *at* relates noun 'room' to noun 'hotel')
We stayed there for a week. (Preposition *for* relates verb 'stayed' to noun 'week')
The place was full of visitors. (Preposition *of* relates adjective 'full' to noun 'visitors')
Everyone was very kind to us. (Preposition *to* relates adjective 'kind' to pronoun 'us')
We were grateful for what they did. (Preposition *for* relates adjective 'grateful' to noun-clause 'what they did')

The noun, pronoun or noun equivalent 'governed by' a preposition is the object of that preposition. It is, therefore, in the accusative case. Nouns in English do not 'inflect' to show that they are accusative. Pronouns (with the exception of 'you' and 'it') do.

The letter was addressed to my husband and me. (*not* 'to. . .I')
She is a writer for whom I have great respect. (*not* 'for who')
There has always been rivalry between Jones and him. (*not* 'between. . .he')

Preposition means 'placed before'. A preposition often precedes the noun, pronoun or noun equivalent that is its object. It can, however, come at the end of a phrase, clause or sentence (exploding the superstitious belief that it must never do so). For example, when a preposition has as its object an 'understood' relative pronoun, the preposition must come at the end.

That is the room we stayed in. ('That is the room in which we stayed')

And a choice is often open, as in these examples, each of which is correctly constructed:

This is the desk which he invariably wrote at.
This is the desk at which he invariably wrote.

The first version is less formal than the second. The choice, as is often the case, is made on grounds of appropriateness not of correctness.

The use of prepositions to introduce phrases was dealt with in Sections 5.7 and 8.4.

12.8 CONJUNCTIONS

Conjunctions are 'joining' words. They link single words together: 'A parent *and* child can travel on one ticket'. They link phrases together: 'A bad journey by rail *or* by road.' They link two main clauses together to form a double sentence: 'I have written *but* I have not had a reply'. They link more than two main clauses together to form a multiple sentence.

A co-ordinating conjunction links co-ordinate clauses: that is, clauses of equal rank. It may link two or more main clauses, as in the example just given. It may link two or more subordinate clauses of equal rank and identical function: for example, two co-ordinate adjective-clauses.

A subordinating conjunction links a subordinate clause to a main clause.

When the orchestra stopped, the audience was silent.
The crowd grew restless *as* the speaker droned on.
It was obvious *that* he had failed.
While we were waiting for our guests to arrive, I wondered *whether* I had prepared enough food.

12.9 INTERJECTIONS

Often found at the beginning of sentences, especially in dialogue, to express feelings or attitudes, interjections play no part in the grammar of a sentence. They may take the form of sounds ('Hm!'); of single words ('Well!'); of phrases ('Oh dear!'); of sentences ('I say!'; 'You know').

12.10 'IT' AS A PROVISIONAL SUBJECT

The idiomatic use of 'it' as a provisional subject should be noted.

It was easy to see where he had gone wrong.
It is unlikely that we shall be back tomorrow.

Those two sentences can be turned round so that 'it' is eliminated. If that is done, their meaning is unchanged, but they are no longer idiomatic.

Where he had gone wrong was easy to see.
That we shall be back tomorrow is unlikely.

In their original and much more acceptable versions, 'where he had gone wrong' and 'that we shall be back tomorrow' are noun-clauses in apposition to the provisional subject 'It"

12.11 'THERE' AS AN INTRODUCTORY ADVERB

'There' is frequently used to introduce a verb (often the verb *to be*) in sentences in which the subject/verb order is inverted: that is, in sentences in which the verb precedes its subject.

There was a big audience for the concert that night.
There is no answer.
There is a car outside.

The subjects of those sentences are: 'a big audience'; 'no answer'; 'a car'.

It is sometimes argued that in such sentences, 'there' is an adverb of place. Since it is not easy to discover *where* 'there' is, the term 'introductory adverb' seems a more illuminating description of 'there'.

CHAPTER 13

COMMON ERRORS AND
DEBATABLE POINTS

13.1 INTRODUCTION

Faulty grammar sets up barriers between speaker and listener, between writer and reader. Those barriers have different shapes, but each is an obstacle across the communicator's path. An ungrammatical use of language (spoken or written) cannot be precise; for that reason, it is always harder to understand than it need be.

Again, grammatical error may result in ambiguity, forcing the listener or reader to puzzle out which of two or more possible meanings is the intended one. At worst, the language used may depart so far from the accepted patterns of word behaviour that comprehension is completely blocked.

The errors discussed and illustrated in this chapter are those that most commonly occur. They are the mistakes that we all make when we:

  (i)   break the rules of agreement and case;
 (ii)   break the rule of proximity;
(iii)   fail to provide the links needed to relate one part of a sentence to another;
(iv)   misunderstand the function in a sentence of an individual word, phrase or clause.

It would be foolish to pretend that there is a grammatical rule to solve every problem. That is why some debatable points are included in this chapter. The great help that grammar gives is that it illuminates the nature of such problems and then - even though it is unable to conquer them by direct assault - shows us the way round them.

13.2 AGREEMENT

Because English is free from most of the inflexions (changes in word-form) that are usual in many other languages, the rules of agreement are uncomplicated. One rule must always be kept: 'The verb agrees with its subject in number and in person'. Generally, this gives little trouble, but there are a few tricky points.

(a) The problem of 'attraction'
When the subject-word is separated from its verb by other nouns of a different number, the verb may be 'attracted' to agree with a word that is not its subject.

Wrong
1 The basket of apples and pears *were* hanging from a hook.
2 Current applications of that useful material, fibreglass, *has* made the designer's task easier.
3 That new stock control system for spare parts which are despatched every day *were* supplied by Datadot and Company.

Right
1 *was* (subject-word: 'basket')
2 *have* (subject-word: 'applications')
3 *was* (subject-word: 'system')

(b) The problem of pronoun subjects
(i) The relative pronoun
The relative pronoun is the subject of the verb in the relative clause. It must be of the same person and number as its antecedent and the verb must agree with it.

Wrong
1 This must be one of the best plays that *has* been staged at Stratford this season.
2 She is the best of several athletes of great promise who *seems* to be out of favour with the selectors.
3 The success of the new branch is one of the recent developments that *justifies* our faith in the company.

Right
1 *have* ('plays that have')
2 *seem* ('athletes who seem')
3 *justify* ('developments that justify')

(ii) Singular pronouns that are sometimes plural
Difficulties arise with the pronouns 'anybody', 'anyone', 'each', 'either', 'everybody', 'everyone', 'neither', 'none'. Usually, they are singular and should be followed by singular verbs (and by singular possessive adjectives).

144

Wrong
1 Each of the candidates *are* well qualified.
2 Neither of those choices *were* attractive.
3 Anyone trying to unravel the complexities of these forms *are* in danger of making mistakes.

Right

1 *is*   ('Each is . . .')
2 *was* ('Neither was . . .')
3 *is*   ('Anyone is . . .')

But things are not always quite so simple. For example, 'everybody', 'everyone', and 'none' may be used in a plural sense. In such instances, 'everybody' and 'everyone' are the equivalent of 'all the people', and 'none' is the equivalent of 'not any'. Commonsense then demands that they are treated as plurals. Their plurality is then reflected by subsequent pronouns and/or possessive adjectives (see example 1, below), as well as by their verbs (see example 2, below).

Examples
1 When the champions' coach returned, *everybody surged* forward to give *their* heroes a frenzied welcome.

In that example, 'everybody' clearly means 'all the waiting people'. The verb-form *surged* is not inflected to show person or number, but it is the verb agreeing with 'everybody'. The possessive adjective *their* is used in preference to 'his' (or 'his or her') to reflect the undoubtedly plural sense of 'everybody'.

2 The new storage system worked so well that, after six months, *none* of the apples *were* rotten.

In that example, 'none' clearly means 'not any'. The verb-form *were* is used in preference to 'was' to reflect the undoubtedly plural sense of 'none'.

(iii) The sex problem: personal pronouns and possessive adjectives
Though not strictly a subject/verb agreement problem, this topic is best dealt with here because it follows on from (ii).

The English language does not possess a 'common gender' personal pronoun. This deficiency causes problems. The standard argument that 'he' includes 'she' (and that 'his' includes 'her') is unconvincing. It certainly does not work in practice.

Often, 'he and/or she' and 'his and/or her' can be used to avoid the absurdities caused by 'he' and 'his'.

Example
The third-year student has a wide choice which *he or she* can exercise in the light of *his or her* second-year results.

The snag is that frequent repetition of 'he and/or she' and 'his and/or her' is clumsy. Other ways out of the difficulty must often be found.

Examples of the problem and possible solutions
1 Everyone wanting to pay by cheque must provide evidence of *his* identity.
(*either*) 'Everyone' = 'all those people' so change '*his* identity' to '*their* identity'.
(*or*) The possessive adjective is not essential, so change 'evidence of his identity' to 'evidence of identity'.
2 A brilliant child may be expected to discover that for *himself*.
(*either*) Change 'for himself' to 'unaided'.
(*or*) Use the plural: 'Brilliant children. . .for themselves'.
3 A boy or girl of average ability needs a year of careful preparation if *he* is to be successful in this examination.
Omit 'if he is to be successful'. Substitute 'to succeed in'.

The difficulties caused by the lack of common gender personal pronouns and possessive adjectives are widespread. The illustrations just given suggest that those difficulties can be solved if the speaker or writer gives some thought to a very real problem, the existence of which is too often ignored.

(c) Collective subjects and their verbs
Is a collective noun singular or plural? This is the basic rule: if we are thinking about the *individual items* composing the group or collection named by the collective noun, we should treat it as a *plural* subject; if we are thinking about the group or collection *as a whole*, as *one*, as an *entity*, we should treat it as a *singular* subject.

Right
1 My family *are* punctual and hard-working people.
2 My family *has* lived in this village for a hundred years.

But we often use a collective noun subject in less clear-cut circumstances than those just illustrated.

Example
Towerbridge Town's football team (is/are) training at Skegthorpe in preparation for the new season.

The team is undoubtedly training as a *whole*, as a single *unit*. That is the argument for singularity. The members of that team are undoubtedly training as *individuals*. That is the argument for plurality. In that example, either a singular or a plural verb may be used.

Once the choice has been made – where choice is permissible – then we must stick to it. We must not chop and change.

Wrong
The government *is* under pressure from *their* supporters to change course. (*Either* 'is/its' *or* 'are/their')

We need to look ahead and try to envisage the consequences of the choice. One or the other may be the easier to sustain through an extended piece of writing. The perils of inconsistency multiply as subsequent subjects and verbs, pronouns and possessive adjectives get caught up in the woolly-minded mess.

Wrong
Towerbridge Town's football team *is* training at Skegthorpe in preparation for the new season. *They* return to Towerbridge on Friday, ready for the first League fixture in which *its* opponents will be Hampton. The London club *informs* our Sports Editor that *they* expect to make an important new signing before *their* match with Towerbridge. *Their* manager says that his team *is* in great form and *have* benefited from new training techniques perfected by *its* coach.

(d) 'Either. . .or. . .'/'neither. . .nor. . .' subjects
The construction involves two subjects and one verb. When both the subject-words are of the same person and number there is no problem.

Right
1 Either Thomas or Brown *is* a suitable choice.
2 Neither the parents nor their children *were* on the bus.

Problems arise when the two subject-words are of different person and number. In such circumstances the rule is that the verb agrees with the *nearer* of the two subject-words.

Right
1 Neither the employees nor their boss *realises* the size of the problem.
2 Either Dr Jenkins or I *am* on call at night.

The rule is a good guide, but the results of applying it are sometimes awkward. In example 1, 'employees' is perhaps far enough removed from 'realises' not to jar. In example 2, 'Dr Jenkins' is too close to 'am' for comfort. The sentence is correct, but it should be recast along these lines: 'Either Dr Jenkins or I can be called out at night'.

Recasting is often the best way of dealing with the problem of 'alternative subjects', for clumsiness – even correct clumsiness – is always to be avoided.

Fortunately, English often permits alternative subjects of different person and number to be followed by a common verb-form.

1 Neither the employees nor their boss *realised* the size of the problem.
2 Either Dr Jenkins or I *must be* on call at night.

(e) Double and multiple subjects
As a rule, double and multiple subjects are plural.

Right
1 Jones, Smith and Brown *are* on the committee.
2 His idealism and devotion to duty *entitle* him to respect.

Some apparently double subjects are so fused by frequent use that they may be treated as singular.

Right
1 Fish and chips *is* not my favourite meal.
2 Pen and ink *has* been displaced by the ballpoint.
3 Bread and water *was* the vagrant's staple diet in prison.

(f) Parenthesis in subjects
The punctuation of what appears to be a double subject may result in a shift of stress on to the first subject-word. Then, instead of the two subject-words being of equal importance, the first becomes of major importance. It is then regarded as a single subject and – if singular – takes a singular verb.

Right
1 The engine, and the special fuel needed for its testing, *was* flown to the proving ground without delay.
2 Truth, and the safeguards that protect it, *is* the first casualty in every war.

Note the importance of the parenthetical commas. If they are omitted, the subject is clearly plural. Note, too, that if an emphasised subject-word is plural, the verb must be plural.

As always, punctuation is an essential element of meaning. It goes hand-in-hand with grammar.

Compare
1 The President, and his wife and children, *was* prominent at the opening ceremony.
2 The President and his wife and children *were* prominent at the opening ceremony.

(g) Appositional words in subjects

Again, punctuation plays a vital part. The appositional words must not be allowed to break subject/verb 'concord' (agreement).

Wrong

1 Three squadrons of cavalry, the miserable remnant of a once-mighty army, *was* surrounded.
2 The treasure, gold bars, pearls and rubies, *were* recovered from the wreck.
3 The residual estate – hall, farms and cottages – *were* inherited by a distant cousin.

Right

1 *were* (subject-word: 'squadrons')
2 *was* (subject-word: 'treasure')
3 *was* (subject-word: 'estate')

(h) The provisional subject 'it'

See Section 12.10. The verb agrees with the provisional subject.

Right

Unless I am much mistaken, it *was* those old fuses that caused the fire.

(i) The introductory adverbs 'here' and 'there'

See Section 12.11. Errors of agreement occur when the introductory adverb is taken to be the subject of the verb.

Wrong

1 Here *is* the armoury, the dungeons, the keep and the drawbridge, all in excellent repair.
2 In the great hall, there *is* a genuine Rembrandt and several lesser portraits.

Right

1 *are* (the subject is multiple: 'the armoury...drawbridge')
2 *are* (the subject is double: 'a genuine Rembrandt...portraits')

(j) Subject/verb/complement balance

Example 2, illustrates the fact that correct grammar can be clumsy. 'There *are* a genuine Rembrandt and several lesser portraits' jars because of the proximity of the plural verb *are* and the very pronounced singularity of *a genuine Rembrandt*.

Clumsiness of this kind results when the subject-word and its complement are of different numbers.

Clumsy but correct
1 The crown jewels *are* a remarkable sight.
2 The main pleasure of his retirement *was* his flowers.
3 What I most miss *is* long walks.

Recasting can usually remove the clumsiness without changing the intended sense.

1 The crown jewels make a remarkable sight.
2 The main pleasure of his retirement was his flower-garden.
3 What I miss most is going for long walks.

13.3 CASE

(a) Nouns

See Section 12.2 (e). The genitive is the only case for which English nouns are inflected. Common errors made in marking the genitive are:

1 The use of the apostrophe in plural nouns that are not possessive.

Wrong
The *cabbage's* on that stall are dear, but the *mushroom's* are reasonable.

Right
cabbages; mushrooms: the nouns are plural, but not genitive

2 Misplacing the apostrophe to mark the genitive case of proper nouns ending with *s*.

Wrong
We are studying *Dicken's* novel, *Our Mutual Friend*, and *Keat's* poetry.

Right
Dickens' (or *Dickens's*) novel; *Keats'* (or *Keats's*) poetry

3 Misplacing the apostrophe to mark the genitive case of nouns that have a special plural form.

Wrong
1 He reached the final round of the *mens'* competition.
2 The *ladie's* changing-room is in the new pavilion.

Right
1 *men's* competition: man – men – men's
2 *ladies'* changing-room: lady – ladies – ladies'

(b) Personal pronouns
The nominative and accusative case-forms are often confused.

Wrong

1 Keep this a secret between you and *I*.

2 There was a long delay at the airport, but in the end they let the B flight passengers through and then *we* who were trying to get on the C flight.

Right

1 *me*: accusative case, object of the preposition 'between'

2 *us*: accusative case, object of the verb 'let'

(c) The interrogative pronouns 'who?' and 'whom?'

The grammatical rule governing the case-form to be used is so often ignored that it is perhaps not a rule any longer. Strictly speaking, 'Who did you see?' and 'Who have you asked?' are wrong. The interrogative pronoun is the object of the verb in both those questions, and '*Whom* did you see?' and '*Whom* have you asked?' are correct. Nowadays, few grammarians would insist on those forms and fewer users of English would employ them. General use is changing the grammar.

(d) The relative pronoun 'who' (nominative) and 'whom' (accusative)

The distinction matters and must be observed. When the pronoun is the subject of the verb *who* must be used. When it is the object of the verb or the object of a preposition *whom* must be used.

Wrong

1 They have chosen the candidate *whom* they think will appeal to the radical voters.

2 They have chosen the candidate *who* they think the radical voters will support.

3 They have chosen the candidate to *who* they think the radical voters will be attracted.

Right

1 *who*: subject of the verb 'will appeal'

2 *whom*: object of the verb 'will support'

3 *whom*: object of the preposition 'to'

(e) Personal pronouns in clauses of comparison

The distinction between nominative and accusative case-forms in comparisons can be vital to the meaning. The omission of the verb in the clause of comparison often misleads. Keep these two examples in mind.

1 They are offering you a bigger salary than *I*.

2 They are offering you a bigger salary than *me*.

The meaning of sentence 1 is: 'They are offering you a bigger salary than I am offering you.'
The meaning of sentence 2 is: 'They are offering you a bigger salary than they are offering me'.

Although the meaning can sometimes be clear when the grammar is wrong, it is better not to get careless about what can be a crucial distinction. We may be in no danger of misunderstanding 'I wish I were as tall as him' ('as *he*' is the correct form), but if we use the correct case-form in such circumstances we are less likely to go wrong when accuracy affects meaning.

(f) Personal pronouns as complements

When the complement refers to the subject it should be in the nominative case-form, but usage is triumphing over grammar. Few English speakers or writers now use the academically correct: 'It is I' or 'That is he'.

(g) Misuse of the emphasising and reflexive pronouns

Not itself a case fault, this error occurs because people are afraid of using the accusative forms of the personal pronouns.

Wrong
1 Seats have been reserved for my mother and *myself*.
2 The reporter seemed keen to interview our neighbours as well as *ourselves*.

Right
1 *me*   (see Section 12.3(b))
2 *us*   (see Section 12.3(b))

(h) The genitive case of the indefinite pronoun 'one'

'One' = 'people in general'; 'anyone'. If you must use it, remember that its genitive form is 'one's (*not* 'his' or 'hers' or 'theirs'). The use of 'one' and 'one's' should be avoided. It sounds stilted or affected, according to the personality of the user. Perfectly adequate (and much more English-sounding) alternatives are always available: 'we' or 'people', for example.

(i) The genitive case of the personal pronouns

The apostrophe is not used to mark the genitive case of the personal pronouns: 'theirs' *not* 'their's'; 'ours' *not* 'our's', and so on. Remember that the possessive form of 'it' is *its*. ('It's' is the contraction of 'it is'.)

13.4 VERB-FORMS

(a) The verbs 'to lay' and 'to lie'

The verb *to lay* should be used transitively. The verb *to lie* should be used intransitively. Remember this example of correct usage: '*Lay* down your weapons and *lie* down beside them'. The principal parts of the two verbs are:

to lay: lay   laid   laid
to lie: lie   lay   lain

Wrong

1 I *was laying* down when the phone rang.
2 The workman *has lain* two hundred bricks already.
3 *Lie* your wet coat on this chair to dry.

Right

1 I *was lying* down   (intransitive)
2 *has laid* two hundred bricks   (transitive)
3 *Lay* your wet coat down   (transitive)

(b) The verbs 'to raise' and 'to rise'

The verb *to raise* should be used transitively. The verb *to rise* should be used intransitively. Correct use: 'The sun *was rising* when we *raised* the blinds'.

The principal parts of the two verbs are:

to raise   raise   raised   raised
to rise   rise   rose   risen

(c) The verb 'to hang'

Errors are made because the verb has two forms of its past simple tense and two forms of its past participle. They are used differently.

to hang   hang   hung   hung
                      hanged   hanged

A coat is *hung* on a hook, but a man is *hanged* on a gallows. *Hanged* is used only in the sense of execution. For all other meanings *hung* is used.

(d) 'may' and 'can'

These two verbs belong to a small group called 'defective verbs' because they lack the full range of tenses and are used only in certain forms. (There is, for example, no infinitive 'to may'. Nor is there a future simple 'I shall can'.) The other defective verbs are: must, ought, shall, will. 'May' and 'can' have different meanings, often confused. The following examples illustrate correct usage:

Right
1 *May* I go to the cinema?
2 You *may*, if you *can* afford to pay for yourself.
3 He *can* play a good game of tennis.
4 We have no firm plans as yet, but we *may* go away in July.
5 The regulations state that we *may* not burn rubbish in the garden.

(e) 'shall/will' and 'should/would'

See Section 12.5(h), where the correct verb-forms are set out. Current misuse of 'shall/will' and 'should/would' blurs distinctions of tense and volition.

(f) Split infinitives

It is best to know what a split infinitive is before condemning it as an error. A split infinitive occurs only when words are placed between *to* and the rest of the infinitive. The infinitives are *not* split in these examples.

Right
1 He deserves to be severely punished.
2 She claims to have only just heard the news.
  There *is* a split infinitive in each of the following examples. They are clumsy errors and could easily have been avoided.

Wrong
1 The government's intention is to speedily and thoroughly restore the balance between exports and imports.
2 Tax burdens are to as quickly we can manage it be reduced.

The rule is that never more than one adverb should be placed between *to* and the rest of the infinitive, and then only when placing it elsewhere causes ambiguity or clumsiness.

13.5 THE RULE OF PROXIMITY

Because the language has so few inflexions to mark the parts of speech and their functions, users of English must pay particular attention to the position and order of sentence items. Individual words and groups of words must be placed as near as possible to the words or groups of words to which they refer. When this common-sense 'rule of proximity' is broken, absurdity, ambiguity or downright nonsense result.

(a) 'Only' must be put in its place

Each of these sentences is grammatically correct, but each gives different information according to the position of 'only'.

1 Only the herb-gardens are open to club members on Sundays.
2 The herb-gardens are open only to club members on Sundays.
3 The herb-gardens are open to club members on Sundays only.

(b) Misplaced adjective-phrases and clauses

1 Old books are always wanted by collectors with leather bindings.
2 After a long search, I found the car I was looking for in a small garage in excellent condition.

(c) Misplaced adverb-phrases and clauses

1 Alarmed by falling sales, the big brewers spent millions to win back beer-drinkers on commercial television and radio.

Where it stands in that sentence 'on commercial television and radio' is an adjective-phrase qualifying the noun 'beer-drinkers'; but it was surely intended to be an adverb-phrase (of place) modifying the verb 'spent'.

2 Jones realised that he had forgotten to renew his licence while driving to work that morning.

In that sentence, 'while driving to work that morning' is a contracted clause with an 'understood' subject and a 'part-understood' verb: 'while (he) (was) driving to work that morning' ('while' is a subordinating conjunction). It is intended to function as a subordinate adverb-clause (of time) and it should be placed near to the main verb 'realised'.

(d) Misrelated participial phrases

The basic fault is the same as that illustrated in paragraphs (b) and (c), above, but this particular manifestation of the error is so common that it demands a section to itself. Phrases of all kinds – participial, prepositional, gerundive and infinitive (see Section 8.4) – must be so positioned in a sentence that their function is clear. Careless placing of participial phrases is the trap into which we most often fall.

Wrong
1 Arriving at the theatre late, the seats we wanted had been taken.
2 Crossing the Clopton Bridge, that view of the town has delighted generations of tourists.
3 Forced to sell in a hurry, the market inflicted heavy losses on the speculator.

Participial phrases (present and past) function as adjectives. They must be so placed in a sentence that there can be no doubt which noun or noun equivalent they are intended to qualify.

(e) Unrelated participial phrases

Rearrangement of sentence order usually corrects the errors caused by *mis*related participial phrases. *Un*related participial phrases present worse problems. A misrelated participial phrase is so placed that it qualifies the wrong noun or noun equivalent. It can be moved into a position in which it can do its proper job. An unrelated participial phrase exists in a grammatical limbo. There is no noun or noun equivalent in the sentence to which it can logically refer. Rearrangement cannot put such a sentence right. It must be rewritten.

Wrong

1 Having considered the high level of interest rates, depressed trading conditions are likely to persist into next year.

2 Not having much mathematical knowledge, statistics can be used to baffle intelligent readers.

Right

1 The high level of interest rates makes it likely that depressed trading conditions will persist into next year.

2 Statistics can be used to baffle intelligent readers who have not much mathematical knowledge.

Do not confuse unrelated participial phrases with the grammatically correct absolute constructions described in Section 12.5(e). An unrelated participial phrase reaches out vainly to qualify a non-existent noun or noun equivalent in the rest of the sentence. The participle in an absolute construction qualifies a noun or noun equivalent inside that construction. That is its job. The absolute construction as a whole does the work of an adverb. It is complete in itself, not tied in any way to the rest of the sentence.

Right

1 All things considered, it was a good result.

2 Considering his injury, he ran a good race.

The comma after the absolute construction marks its grammatical independence.

13.6 WOOLLY USE OF PRONOUNS

(a) 'This', 'that', 'these', 'those' as pointers

The demonstrative pronouns demonstrate or 'point out'. They must be used so that they point clearly and unambiguously to a particular noun or noun equivalent.

156

Wrong

1 A new wave of English composers has arrived with the publication of the Maldon Group's song cycles in Johnson's latest collection, and *this* is certain to be regarded as a landmark. (Exactly *what* is certain to be regarded as a landmark?)

2 The qualities revealed are likely to have repercussions among younger writers who regard the Maldon Group as their mentors, but *these* will come under critical scrutiny. (Exactly *what* or *who* will come under critical scrutiny?)

In neither of those sentences has the demonstrative pronoun been provided with an identifiable 'target'.

(b) The dangers of 'it'
A carelessly-used 'it' is as confusing as a badly-chosen and misplaced pointer. The following passage illustrates the dangers of using 'it' and the demonstratives in a woolly-minded way:

Wrong
The chairman described the company's position and prospects. Production had been low, owing to technical problems, and sales had fallen. *It* had been a matter of concern, but *it* should soon improve. *This* accounted for the poor profits in the past six months. The setback had been severe, but temporary, he was sure, and conditions were improving. Shareholders should bear *that* in mind when reading the accounts and studying results. *These* should change dramatically.

(c) Personal pronouns with ambiguous reference

Wrong
1 The champion's business manager told our reporter that *he* was furious with *him*. (*Who* was furious with *whom*?)
2 My supporters have never encouraged violent attacks on our opponents and I am in agreement with *them* (In agreement with *whom* or with *what*?)

13.7 DEFINING AND NON-DEFINING PHRASES AND CLAUSES

There is a difference in meaning between a defining phrase or clause and a non-defining phrase or clause. This difference must be marked by correct punctuation.

Compare
1 (Defining phrase) Cars *with front-wheel drive* are noted for their road-holding qualities.
2 (Defining clause) People over sixty *who are entitled to half-price travel* should apply by 1 October.
3 (Non-defining phrase) Cars, *with all their advantages*, make big demands on scarce supplies of fuel.
4 (Non-defining clause) The main road, *which carries a lot of traffic*, passes through some pretty villages.

Use commas to mark off non-defining phrases and clauses. Do not mark off defining phrases and clauses.

Compare
1 (Defining clause) We have studied the diet of islanders who were aged between 13 and 21 on 1 January last.
2 (Non-defining clause) Our investigation has been funded by the Universal Trust, which takes a keen interest in dietary problems.

Remember that a non-defining phrase or clause adds to the meaning of (describes) its antecedent, but it does not constitute a vital element of its identity. A defining phrase or clause positively identifies its antecedent and marks it off from all the others of its class. Cars with front-wheel drive are different from other cars.

13.8 CHOPPING AND CHANGING

Avoid sudden shifts of voice, tense, and person within sentences.

Wrong
1 As soon as the mechanics had traced the fault, the necessary repairs were begun by them.
2 Customers reported a weakness in the design of the gearbox, saying that you had difficulty in changing down.
3 By now, the audience was bored and they lose patience with the long-winded speaker.

Right
1 Avoid shift of voice (. . .they *began* the necessary repairs. . .)
2 Avoid shift of person (. . .*they* had difficulty. . .)
3 Avoid shift of tense (. . .they *lost* patience. . .)

158

13.9 TESTS

Test 51
Answers on page 173.
Correct the error in each of the following sentences.

1 There are on this estate, between the houses and the blocks of flats, a fine example of open spaces planted with lawns and trees.
2 The unrest underlying these disagreements call for investigation.
3 This is one of the best horses that has been bred in England in the past ten years.
4 It is no trouble at all to John and Kate and I to take it in turns to bring you books from the library.
5 Being tone-deaf the superb woodwind made no different impression on James than a badly-played penny-whistle would have done.
6 The kitchen needs painting badly and I must get it done.
7 If they refuse to help with the chores us others must do them on our own.
8 My firm has not yet decided whether I will be sent to Singapore next year.
9 Being tired after a long journey, I went up to my room to have a lay down before dinner.
10 Although Jackson was the heaviest, Peters packed a more powerful punch and this gave him victory.
11 To avoid excessive tyre wear it is necessary to frequently – at least once a week – check pressures.
12 If, as may well be the case, you find that raw meat upsets your dog, boil it.

Test 52 (Revision)
Answers on page 173.
Pick out the noun-clause in each of the following and describe its function.

1 Where the stolen horse had been hidden could only be surmised.
2 I really cannot divulge what was told to me in confidence.
3 The police tried to discover where the weapon had been bought.
4 My theory is that they will leave the country by air.
5 The radio broadcast the news that the government had fallen.

Test 53 (Revision)
Answers on page 173.
Pick out the adjective-clause in each of the following and describe its function.

1 The methods which the party used to secure a majority in the election were widely condemned.

2 These are the works of art he created during his brief but brilliant life.

3 I very much wish to live in a city where there are theatres and art galleries.

4 The information that they received at midnight enabled the police to make an arrest early the next morning.

5 The debating society, which meets on Mondays at 5.30, is trying to recruit more members from the first-year students.

(Note the punctuation of sentence 5 and compare it with the punctuation of sentence 1.)

Test 54 (Revision)
Answers on page 173.
Pick out the adverb-clause in each of the following and describe its kind and function.

1 Whenever I try to work at home somebody switches on the television.

2 The rebels always attacked where they were least expected to do so.

3 Because his conversation was tiring his patient, the doctor fell silent.

4 Throughout his working life he saved money so that his old age would be comfortable.

5 The prisoner leapt into the air as if he had been stung.

6 We ran faster than our rivals had done the day before.

7 After a term of comparative idleness he worked so hard in the last week or so that he came top in the examination.

8 I shall have to deal severely with you if you are late for work again.

9 The book did not sell well although the critics praised it.

10 At last night's concert he played the sonata as brilliantly as he has ever done.

ANSWERS TO TESTS

Test 1, page 6.
1 s. 2 p. 3 s. 4 p. 5 s. 6 s. 7 p. 8 s. 9 s. 10 s. 11 s. 12 p. 13 p. 14 s.

Test 2, page 6.
1 Their new car was parked at the end of the street.
2 Radio reception is poor after dark.
3 We took it in turns to keep watch.
4 Through a silly mistake, I was given the wrong number.
5 Desperate men proceed by violent means.
6 Judging by the results, there was a fault in the circuit.
7 Those books were borrowed without permission.
8 No more aid is available for the present.

Test 3, page 7.
1 s. 2 s. 3 q. 4 c. 5 s. 6 e. 7 s. 8 q. 9 s. 10 s.

Test 4, page 7.
Topic sewing
  (i)   This machine has several new attachments.
 (ii) Are they worth the money?
(iii) Try them.
(iv) Excellent!

Topic cooking
  (i)   It's a good recipe.
 (ii) How do you know?
(iii) Taste this pastry.
(iv) What an improvement it is!

Topic reading
  (i)   Slow reading is a handicap.
 (ii) What can I do about it?
(iii) Take a rapid-reading course.
(iv) What good ideas you have!

Test 5, page 8.
1 The film was a good one. It kept closely to the facts of the historical events on which it was based.

2 By half-time it was clear that we were going to win. Our forwards were stronger and faster than theirs.
3 On a very cold morning, frost crystals appear on the windows. Their beauty is some compensation for our discomfort.
4 The bus was late in starting. We missed morning assembly that day.
5 The beech keeps its leaves longer than most other trees. Its autumn colours last well into winter. Often they are still there in early spring.

Test 6, page 8.
Do you understand the difference between sentences and phrases? It is important to be clear about it. Making complete sense depends on being able to frame sentences. Think hard about punctuation, too. This passage is not easy to understand. Why isn't it? It's a jumble! The writer has forgotten to punctuate.

Test 7, page 13.

Subject	Predicate
1 This test	is the seventh in this book
2 Most readers	will have no trouble in answering
3 Studying sentences	is the main activity of grammar
4 Subject and predicate	must be identified
5 The term 'predicate'	comes from a Latin word meaning 'to declare'

Test 8, page 13.
1 The test pilot reached a record-breaking speed.
2 A nursing auxiliary examined my swollen hand.
3 The explorers were exhausted after their polar journey.
4 An amateur astronomer identified the comet.
5 International observers tried to arrange a cease-fire.

Test 9, page 13.
1 The first day of the new term was chaotic.
2 The Suez Canal is a vital waterway.
3 Grammatical errors impede communication.
4 Malaria has ceased to be a mysterious illness.
5 Air travel is still very expensive.

Test 10, page 16.
3 *Subject*   (You)
  Predicate   don't touch that switch
4 *Subject*   (You)
  Predicate   be careful
5 *Subject*   (You)
  Predicate   keep quiet

162

Test 11, page 17.
Sentences: 2 s. 3 c. 4 q. 6 s. 7 c. 8 s. 9 q. 10 e.

Test 12, page 17.
1 What would you like for your birthday?
2 What kind of a book would you like?
3 Would you like a book of short stories?
4 When does your train leave?
5 Why were they late?

Test 13, page 17.
1 Down!
2 Keep cool!
3 Look after it.
4 Tickets, please!
5 Be careful crossing the street.

Test 14, page 18.

	Subject	Predicate
1	Horace	hit his hand with a hammer
2	Tuesday night's programmes	are better than Wednesday's
3	he	With a courage born of desperation flung himself at his enemies
4	they	Slowly and painfully worked out the answers
5	(You)	are happy
6	(You)	put it down
7	(You)	(are) happy
8	(You)	Have cleaned your shoes
9	Reading	is one of my favourite pleasures
10	Jean	has used the last of the shampoo

Test 15, page 21.
1 *park*
You can *park* in this street after six o'clock.
The *park* is looking very pretty now.
2 *down*
We walked across the *down* before breakfast.
I ran *down* the hill to meet him.
3 *colour*
Green is not a *colour* that she ought to wear.
Colour all the woodwork black.

4 *knife*
The wind had a *knife* edge yesterday.
Lend me your *knife*, please.
5 *break*
If that trays slips it will *break* the teapot.
I mugged up the facts in the morning *break*.

Test 16, page 24.

Proper nouns	Common nouns
1 Henry	runs day
2 Southampton July England	car
3 Hodge	cat
4 Dickens	novel
5 Tuesday	birthday year

Test 17, page 24.
The nouns are: son, rooms, hospital, days, fears, satisfaction, youth, plague, fever, remedies. They are all common nouns, except 'satisfaction' and 'fears', which are abstract nouns.

Test 18, page 25.

Common nouns	Abstract nouns
1 engine revolutions	quietness
2 friends relations	solitude
3 player	sportsmanship
4 rivals	enmity
5	beauty

Test 19, page 25.
1 navy. 2 committee. 3 flocks, 4 kit. 5 shoals.

Test 20, page 25.
Proper noun'   Smith
Abstract noun: courage
Collective noun: team
Common nouns: friend member cup

Test 21, page 28.
1 untied. 2 must have opened. 3 appeared to be. 4 was revising. 5 upset.

Test 22, page 28.
Remember, question sentences are converted into statements before being analysed. For example, 'Have you finished that book?' is converted into 'You have finished that book'.

Subject	Verb
1 you	Have finished
2 ten new candidates	were accepted
3 you	will be
4 A lecturer in engineering	should lack
5 We	need keep

Test 23, page 30.
The pronouns are: I, they, me, you, everyone, this, it, everything.

Test 24, page 32.
1 *many* qualifies 'people'.
2 *this* and *hot* qualify 'room'.
3 *what* qualifies 'colour'.
4 *my* qualifies 'pen'; *empty* qualifies 'yours'.
5 *their* and *splendid* qualify 'house'
6 *twenty* and *later* qualify 'chapters'; *that* qualifies 'character'; *his* qualifies 'book'.
7 *dwarf* qualifies 'tulips'; *this* qualifies 'soil'.
8 *our* and *fancy* qualify 'dress'.
9 *their* and *kind* qualify 'hostess'; *delicious* qualifies 'meal'.
10 *his* qualifies 'record'; *ten* qualifies 'years'.

Test 25, page 37.
1 *long* modifies verb 'wait'.
2 *exceptionally* modifies adjective 'good'.
3 *unwillingly* modifies verb 'answered'; *rather* modifies adverb 'unwillingly'.
4 *where* modifies verb 'are going'.
5 *slowly* modifies verb 'rose'; *very* modifies adverb 'slowly'.
6 *down* modifies verb 'keep'.
7 *why* modifies verb 'agree'; *amicably* modifies verb 'agree'.
8 *little* modifies verb 'said'; *much* modifies verb 'suffered'.
9 *well* modifies verb 'get'; *quickly* modifies verb 'get'.
10 *by* modifies verb 'go'; *fast* modifies verb 'go'; *so* modifies adverb 'fast'.

Test 26, page 37.
1 *last* is an adverb modifying the verb 'came'.
2 *last* is an adjective qualifying the noun 'horse'.
3 *easy* is an adjective qualifying the noun 'test'.
4 *easy* is an adverb modifying the verb 'felt'.
5 *still* is an adjective qualifying the noun 'winds'.

6 *still* is an adverb modifying the verb 'is trying'.
7 *too* is an adjective qualifying the pronoun 'she'.
8 *too* is an adverb modifying the verb 'bring'.
9 *monthly* is an adverb modifying the verb 'collected'.
10 *monthly* is an adjective qualifying the noun 'cheque'.

Test 27, page 41.

	Preposition	Prepositional phrase	Function
1	underneath	underneath the grey stone	adverb-phrase modifying verb 'was buried'
2	with	with your decision	adverb-phrase modifying adjective 'happy'
3	of	of rubble	adjective-phrase qualifying noun 'heap'
4	from	from that school	adjective-phrase qualifying noun 'candidates'
5	of	of their football team	adverb-phrase modifying adjective 'proud'
6	on	on a postcard	adjective-phrase qualifying noun 'answers'
7	at	at six o'clock	adverb-phrase modifying verb 'was broadcast'
8	from	from the final	adverb-phrase modifying verb 'withdrew'
	because of	because of his injury	adverb-phrase modifying verb 'withdrew'
9	in place of	in place of the minister	adverb-phrase modifying verb 'was sent'
10	in	in that poor soil	adverb-phrase modifying verb 'grows'

Test 28, page 47.

	Subject		Predicate	
	subject-word	*adjectives or adjective-phrases*	*verb*	*rest of predicate*
1	train	the last	leaves	at midnight
2	revolver	a with a pearl handle	provided	a vital clue
3	books	those on that shelf in the library	are	not often read
4	I		could see	in the background several familiar faces
5	(You)		use	that big spanner

Notes
Sentence 3: 'not' is the 'adverb of negation' modifying the verb 'are'.
Sentence 4: 'in the background' is an adverb-phrase modifying the verb 'could see'.
Sentence 5: is a command-sentence, and the subject-word '(You)' is placed in brackets in the analysis to show that it is 'understood'.

Test 29, page 50.

	Direct object-word	Qualifying word(s)
1	Polonius	–
2	island	the deserted
3	–	–
4	shore	another
5	eyes	their
6	lesson	a hard
7	–	–
8	–	–
9	–	–
10	round	every

Test 30, page 50.

Subject		Predicate			
subject-word	adjectives or adjective-phrases	verb	adverbs or adverb-phrases	direct object-word	adjectives or adjective-phrases
1 pictures	old	make	often at auctions	prices	big
2 prison	this grim	held	in the early 18th century	captives	many unfortunate
3 space		yields	slowly	secrets	its

Test 31, page 51.
1 the institute. 2 the sports club. 3 the audience. 4 the greedy vendor.
5 me.

Test 32, page 54.
1 *notorious*: predicative adjective completing the sense of the verb
'became' and referring to the same person as the subject-word 'he'; *for his
crimes*: adverb-phrase modifying the predicative adjective 'notorious'.
2 *contented*: predicative adjective completing the sense of the verb
'appeared' and referring to the same person as the subject-word 'man'.
3 *good*: predicative adjective completing the sense of the verb 'are' and
referring to the same thing as the subject-word 'sweets'; *for you*: adverb-
phrase modifying the predicative adjective 'good'.
4 *sinister*: predicative adjective completing the sense of the verb 'looks'
and referring to the same thing as the subject-word 'house'; *very*: adverb
modifying the predicative adjective 'sinister'.
5 *greedy*: predicative adjective completing the sense of the verb 'shall
seem' and referring to the same person as the subject-word 'I'.

Test 33, page 54.

Verb	Adverbs or adverb-phrases modifying verb	Direct object-word	Adjectives or adjective-phrases qualifying direct object-word	Indirect object-word	Adjectives or adjective-phrases qualifying indirect object-word	Predicative word + words qualifying or modifying predicative word
1 sang		song	its melancholy			
2 is						cure + a for indigestion
3 did invent		cure	a for indigestion			
4 caused		famine	the worst in the history of that country			
5 finished	at nine o'clock	novel	the			
6 gave	in the night	drink	a from his flask	prisoner	the wakeful	

168

Test 34, page 64.

1 The infinitive *to climb* is the subject of the verb 'requires'. It functions as a noun.

2 The infinitive *to start* modifies the adjective 'ready'. It functions as an adverb.

3 The infinitive *to return* is the object of the verb 'wanted'. It functions as a noun.

4 The infinitive to declare qualifies the pronoun 'anything' It functions as an adjective.

5 The infinitive *to work* is the subject of the verb 'is'. It functions as a noun. The infinitive *to pray* functions as a predicative noun completing the sense of the verb 'is'.

Test 35, page 65.

1 Gerund. Subject of verb 'is'; functions as a noun.

2 Present participle. Qualifies pronoun 'He'; functions as adjective.

3 Present participle. Qualifies noun 'children'; functions as adjective.

4 Gerund. It is the noun in the prepositional phrase 'for its thieving', which functions as an adverb-phrase modifying the predicative adjective 'notorious'.

5 Gerund. It is the noun in the prepositional phrase 'for harvesting', which functions as an adverb-phrase modifying the predicative adjective 'ripe'.

Test 36, page 65.

1 *Alarmed by the trade figures*: adjective-phrase (qualifies noun 'government').

2 *Sleeping so near the road*: adjective-phrase (qualifies pronoun 'I').

3 *reading the six o'clock news*: adjective-phrase (qualifies noun 'announcer').

4 *Tired of waiting*: adjective-phrase (qualifies noun 'crowd').

5 *posted by my mother*: adjective-phrase (qualifies noun 'parcel').

Test 37, page 76.

1

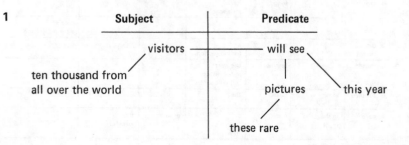

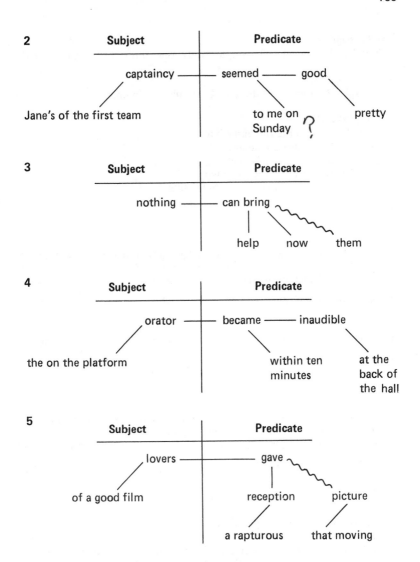

2

Subject	Predicate
captaincy —— seemed —— good	
Jane's of the first team	to me on Sunday ? pretty

3

Subject	Predicate
nothing —— can bring	
	help now them

4

Subject	Predicate
orator —— became —— inaudible	
the on the platform	within ten minutes at the back of the hall

5

Subject	Predicate
lovers —— gave	
of a good film	reception picture
	a rapturous that moving

Test 38, page 84.

1 Double sentence. Two finite verbs: 'was closed' and 'know'; two main clauses: 'The path. . .ago' and 'I. . .in'; link: 'but'.

2 Simple sentence. One finite verb: 'will see'.

3 Double sentence. Two finite verbs: 'leads' and 'must be'; two main clauses: 'The stile. . .track' and 'you. . .it'; link: 'and'.

4 Simple sentence. One finite verb: 'will lead'.

5 Double sentence. Two finite verbs: 'is' and 'will reward'; two main clauses: 'The route. . .find' and 'following. . .district'; link: 'but'.

Test 39, page 86.
1 double. 2 multiple. 3 simple (only one finite verb: 'authorised').

Test 40, page 87.
1 multiple. 2 double. 3 double. 4 simple. 5 complex.

Test 41, page 91.
1 (politicians) who toe the party line.
2 (cars) that have diesel engines.
3 (route) that you recommended.
4 (excuses) which were not convincing.
5 (directories) from which pages are missing.

Test 42, page 94.

	Adjective-clause	Introducing/linking word	Antecedent
1	that I had placed on the table	that	book
2	who found the wallet	who	boy
3	whom I have enjoyed	whom	author
4	which he has begun	which	work
5	(that) I saw	(that)	play

Test 43, page 99.
1 'Though the peasant promised to show them the way through the swamp' modifies the verb 'trust' in the main clause.
2 'where he could watch him closely' modifies the verb 'march' in the main clause.
3 'after they had been on the move for an hour' modifies the verb 'ordered' in the main clause.
4 'If they treated him like this' modifies the verb 'would (not) act' in the main clause.
5 'though some of them pitied the old man' modifies the verb 'felt' in the subordinate clause.
6 'that none of the rebels felt inclined to interfere' modifies the verb 'was' (complement: 'so great') in the main clause.
7 'as their leader decreed' modifies the verb 'march' in the main clause.
8 'as all the others of his tribe had proved to be' modifies the verb 'was' (complement: 'as untrustworthy') in the main clause.

Test 44, page 100.
1 'until we could buy a new car': adverb-clause of time modifying verb 'saved'.
2 'where they had relatives': adjective-clause qualifying noun 'village'.
3 'where he was born': adverb-clause of place modifying verb 'lived'.
4 'where you will find some bargains': adjective-clause qualifying noun 'shop'.

5 'after the announcement was made': adverb-clause of time modifying verb 'left'.

Test 45, page 104.
1 'that they could win the cup': direct object of verb 'think'.
2 'How they are going to do it': subject of verb 'is'.
3 'what their plans are': direct object of verb 'tell'.
4 'that his resignation is expected': in apposition to noun 'rumour'.
5 'that he will resign': object of present participle 'denying', which qualifies noun 'statement'.
6 'who is in control': object of preposition 'on'.
7 'what the facts are': object of infinitive 'to discover'.
8 'what the club hoped for at the beginning of the season': complement of verb 'is''

Test 46, page 104.
1 'When Bunbury first presented himself as a candidate': subordinate adverb-clause (of time) modifying verb 'were'.
2 'that their idol had clay feet': subordinate noun-clause, direct object of verb 'realised'.
3 'who were present': subordinate adjective-clause qualifying pronoun 'Several'; 'that the performance was a great success': subordinate noun-clause, direct object of verb 'assured'.
4 'When we arrived': subordinate adverb-clause (of time) modifying verb 'was'; 'who was in a state of shock': subordinate adjective-clause qualifying noun 'servant'.
5 'unless you have a good reason for staying up late': subordinate adverb-clause (of condition) modifying verb 'should go'.

Test 47, page 113.

		Clause	Kind	Function	Link
1	A	I will certainly lend you my car	Main		
	B	but I must warn you	Main	Co-ordinate with A	but
	a¹	if you want it	Subordinate adverb-clause (of condition)	modifies verb *lend* in A	if
	b¹	that it is not very reliable	subordinate noun-clause	object of verb *warn* in B	that
		Sentence type: double			

Test 47, page 113 (cont)

		Clause	Kind	Function	Link
2	A	This is the place	Main		
	a¹	where I sat	Subordinate adjective-clause	qualifies noun *place* in A	where
	a²	when I was a schoolboy, forty years ago	subordinate adverb-clause (of time)	modifies verb sat in a¹	when
		Sentence type: complex			
3	A	he refused	Main		
	a¹	Although they begged Jenkins to continue as secretary	Subordinate adverb-clause (of concession)	modifies verb *refused* in A	Although
	a²	because he had a lot of work to do	Subordinate adverb-clause (of reason)	modifies verb *refused* in A	because
	a³	and (because) (he) was very tired	Subordinate adverb-clause (of reason)	modifies verb *refused* in A: co-ordinate with a²	and (because)
		Sentence type: complex			
4	A	Just after the discovery of the weapon, a magistrate was found murdered	Main		
	a¹	who had been distinguished by his independent spirit	Subordinate adjective-clause	qualifies noun *magistrate* in A	who
	a²	and who had taken the deposition of the informer	Subordinate adjective-clause	qualifies noun *magistrate* in A: co-ordinate with a¹	and who
		Sentence type: complex			

Test 48, page 113.
1 By chance, I discovered the information that nobody had wanted to give me and I felt better then.
2 Because they wanted to throw the police off the scent, the gang abandoned the stolen car twenty miles away from the scene of the crime.
3 (i) They made a neat parcel of the books *that I chose.*
   (ii) My aunt insisted *that I chose.*
   (iii) Demanding *that I chose*, she refused to take decisions for me.

Test 49, page 113.
1 The papers carried the news *that his illness was serious.*
2 *So that I could finish the job on time* I worked seven days a week for six months.
3 The government used its majority to push through legislation *that was hastily drafted* and *(that) reflected a doctrinaire approach to national problems.*

Test 50, page 114.
1 complex. 2 simple. 3 complex. 4 double. 5 multiple. 6 double.
7 double. 8 multiple.

Test 51, page 158.
1 There *is*...a fine example....
2 The unrest...*calls.*...
3 ...that *have* been bred....
4 ...to John and Kate and *me.*...
5 ...on James, *who was tone-deaf.*...
6 ...*badly needs* painting....
7 ...*we* others must do them....
8 ...whether I *shall* be sent....
9 ...a *lie* down....
10 ...the *heavier.*...
11 ...*to check* pressures frequently – at least once a week.
12 Rewrite the sentence and save the dog!

Test 52, page 158.
1 'where...hidden': subject of verb 'could be surmised'.
2 'what...confidence': object of verb 'divulge'.
3 'where...bought': object of infinitive 'to discover'.
4 'that...air': complement of verb 'is'.
5 'that...fallen': in apposition to object-word 'news'.

Test 53, page 158.
1 'which...election': qualifies noun 'methods'.
2 '(that) he created...life': qualifies noun 'works'.
3 'where...galleries': qualifies noun 'city'.
4 'that...midnight': qualifies noun 'information'.
5 'which...5.30': qualifies noun 'society'.

Test 54, page 159.
1 'Whenever... home': adverb-clause of time modifying phrasal verb 'switches on'.

2 'where...so': adverb-clause of place modifying verb 'attacked'.
3 'Because...patient: adverb-clause of reason or cause modifying verb 'fell'.
4 'so...comfortable': adverb-clause of purpose modifying verb 'saved'.
5 'as...stung': adverb-clause of manner modifying verb 'leapt'.
6 'than...before': adverb-clause of comparison modifying verb 'ran'.
7 'that...examination': adverb-clause of result or consequence modifying verb 'worked'.
8 'if...again': adverb-clause of condition modifying verb 'deal'.
9 'although...it': adverb-clause of concession modifying verb 'sell'.
10 'as...done': adverb-clause of extent or degree modifying verb 'played'.

INDEX

absolute construction   128, 155
abstract noun   23, 116
accusative case   117, 139
active voice   129
adjective   30, 46, 121
  definition   30, 121
  degrees of comparison   123
  kinds of   31, 121 (demonstrative   31, 122; descriptive 31, 121; interrogative   122; number or quantity   31, 122; possessive   31, 121; relative 94, 122)
  position of   31
adjective-clause   90
adjective-phrase   46, 76
  misplaced   154
adjective and adverb   36
adjective and pronoun   32
adverb   33, 137
  definition   35, 137
  degrees of comparison   138
  kinds of   33, 137 (degree or extent   33, 137; interrogative 34, 137; manner   33, 137; number   34, 137; place   33, 137; relative   44, 137; simple 137; time   33, 137)
adverb-clause   95
  of comparison   99
  of concession   99
  of condition   99
  of degree or extent   99
  of manner   98
  of place   98
  of purpose   98
  of reason or cause   98
  of result or consequence   98
  of time   98
adverb-phrase   76, 79
  misplaced   154
adverb and adjective   36
adverb and preposition   40
agreement   124, 142
analysis   68
  descriptive   69
  graphic   72

of complex sentences   105
of double sentences   110
of multiple sentences   110
of phrases   76
of simple sentences   68
  tabular   68
antecedent   94, 143
apostrophe   118, 149, 151
apposition   70, 103, 148
article   32
  definite and indefinite   32, 46
'attraction', problem of   143

balance, subject/verb/complement 148

case   117, 149
  accusative   117, 149
  dative   118
  genitive   118, 149, 151
  nominative   117
  vocative   117
clause   82
  adjective   90
  adverb   95
  co-ordinate   83
  defining and non-defining   156
  main (independent)   83
  noun   101
  subordinate (dependent)   89
clause and sentence   82
collective noun   24, 116
collective subject   145
command sentence   7
  subject of   15
common noun   23, 116
complement (predicative word/s) 52, 68
complex sentence   86
conjunction   41, 140
  co-ordinating   42, 83, 140
  definition   42, 140
  subordinating   98, 140

defining phrase and clause   156
definite article   32, 46

demonstrative pronoun misused 155
dependent (subordinate) clause 89
direct object 48, 53
  direct object-word 48
  word/s qualifying direct object-
    word 49
double sentence 83
double subject 147

exclamation sentence 7
  subject and predicate of 16
  'understood' subject of 16

finite verb 56

gender 118
genitive case 118, 149, 151
gerund 60, 127
gerundive phrase 65, 78
graphic analysis 72

imperative mood 135
imperfect (continuous) tense 131
indefinite article 32, 46
indicative mood 135
indirect object 50
  indirect object-word 51
  word/s qualifying indirect object-
    word 51
infinitive 59, 126
  split 153
infinitive phrase 66, 77
interjection 42, 140
intransitive verb 49, 125
'it'
  as misplaced 'pointer' 156
  as provision subject 140

main (independent) clause 83
mood 135
  imperative 135
  indicative 135
  infinitive 135
  subjunctive 136
multiple sentence 85
multiple subject 147

nominative case 117, 150
non-defining phrase and clause 156
non-finite verb 58, 126
  gerund 60, 127

infinitive 59, 126
  participle, past 62, 128
  participle, present 62, 128
noun 23, 116
  apostrophe in 118, 149
  case 117, 149
  definition 23, 116
  gender 118
  kinds of 23, 116 (abstract
    23, 116; collective 23, 116;
    common 23, 116; proper
    23, 116)
  number 57, 116
  possessive 118
noun-clause 101
  as object of preposition 102
  as object of finite verb 102
  as object of non-finite verb 103
  as subject of verb 101
  in apposition 103
noun-phrase 76
number 58, 116

object 48
  direct 48
  indirect 50
  of non-finite verb 118
  of preposition 117
object-word 49
objective (accusative) case 117, 139
objective complement 53, 68

parenthesis in subject 147
participial phrase 63, 77
  misrelated 154
  unrelated 155
participle 62
  past 62, 128
  present 62, 128
passive voice 129
person 57, 117
phrasal verbs 136
phrase 4, 76
  adjective-phrase 46, 76
  adverb-phrase 76, 79
  gerundive phrase 65, 78
  infinitive phrase 66, 77
  participial phrase 63, 77
  prepositional phrase 38, 41, 77
possessive (genitive) case 118, 149,
  151

predicate   12, 47, 50, 52
  definition   12
  direct object   48
  indirect object   50
  objective complement   53
  predicative word/s (complement)
    52
  verb   25
  word/s modifying verb   47
preposition   38, 139
  as relating/linking word   39, 139
  compound   40
  definition   38
  object of   139
prepositional phrase   38, 41, 77
preposition and adverb   40
pronoun   29, 119
  as complement   151
  as object of preposition   139, 150
  as object of verb   150
  as subject of verb   143
  case   119, 149
  definition   29, 119
  kinds of   119 (demonstrative
    120; emphasising   119, 151;
    indefinite   151; interrogative
    120, 150; number or quantity
    121; personal   119, 149, 150;
    possessive   119, 151; reflexive
    120, 151)
  relative   94, 120, 150
pronoun and adjective   32
proper noun   23, 116
proximity, rule of   153
punctuation   8, 70, 157

question sentence   7
  subject and predicate in   15

relative adjective   94, 122
relative adverb   94, 137
relative pronoun   94, 150

sentence   5, 82
  complex   86 (analysis   105;
    definition   87)
  definition   10
  double   83 (analysis   105;
    definition   84)

kinds of   7 (command   7;
    exclamation   7; question   7;
    statement   7)
  multiple   85 (analysis   105;
    definition   85)
  one-word sentence   16
  punctuation   8
  simple   44, 54 (analysis   68;
    definition   44; parts of   54)
sentence and clause   82
sentence and phrase   5
'shall'/'will'   134, 153
'should'/'would'   134, 153
subject   12
  definition   12
  'either ... or'/'neither ... nor'
    subject   146
  'understood'   15
subject and predicate   10, 12, 45
subject and verb   27, 142
subject/predicate order   13
subject-word   45
  word/s qualifying subject-word
    46
subjective (nominative) case   117,
    150
subjective complement   68
subjunctive mood   136
subordinate (independent) clause
    89

tense   130
  continuous (imperfect)   131
  future   130 (future continuous
    132; future continuous in the
    past   132; future perfect   133;
    future perfect in the past   133;
    future simple   132; future
    simple in the past   132)
  past   130 (past continuous   132;
    past perfect   133; past simple
    132)
  perfect (completed)   131
  present   130 (present continuous
    132; present perfect   132;
    present simple   132)
  simple   130
'there' as introductory adverb   141
transitive verb   48, 125

verb 25, 124
  active and passive 129
  agreement with subject 57, 142
  definition 27, 124
  defective 152
  finite 56
  how to find the verb 27
  infinitive 59, 126
  intransitive 49, 125
  'may' and 'can' 152
  mood 135 (imperative 135;
    indicative 135; infinitive
    135; subjunctive 136)
  multiple-word verb 27
  non-finite 58, 126 (gerund
    60, 127; infinitive 59, 127;
    past participle 62, 129;
    present participle 62, 128)

number 57, 124
object of 48
of incomplete predication 125
person 57, 124
phrasal 136
principal parts of 134
subject of 25, 57, 142
tense 130
'to hang' 152
'to lay' and 'to lie' 152
'to raise' and 'to rise' 152
transitive 48, 125
voice 129

'will'/'shall' 134, 153
'would'/'should' 134, 153